FALL TO PIECES

Stand, Break and Rise

Fall to Pieces
Edited & Compiled by Sonali Sharma
Paperback Edition

First published in India in 2023 by

Inkfeathers Publishing
Vivek Vihar, New Delhi 110095
www.inkfeathers.com

ISBN 978-93-90882-94-6

Copyrights owned by authors of each published write-up within this book.

FALL TO PIECES

Stand, Break and Rise

Edited & Compiled by

Sonali Sharma

Inkfeathers Publishing

www.inkfeathers.com

DISCLAIMER

The anthology "Fall To Pieces" is a collection of 16 short stories and 19 articles written by 24 authors who belong to different parts of the world.

Unless otherwise indicated, all the names, characters, objects, businesses, places, events, incidents—whether physical/non-physical, real/unreal, tangible/ intangible in whatsoever description used in this book are either the product of the author's imagination or used in a fictitious manner. Any resemblance to actual persons, objects, entities, living or dead, or actual events is purely coincidental.

The contents published in this book are solely owned by their respective authors and are in no way intended to hurt anyone's religious, political, spiritual, brand, personal or fanatic beliefs and/or faith, whatsoever. In case, any sort of plagiarism is detected in the contents within this anthology or in case of any complaints, grievances, or objections, neither the anthology editor nor the publisher is to be held responsible.

To Men, Women, & Children

Who are the members

of the

Brave,

Opinionated,

Changemaker

Circle of the Society,

I Proffer the following pages

Featuring the writings of

Aruna Parandhama, Irene Munyiri, *Dr. Janki Mistry,*
Akhila Mohan CG, V. Rashmi Rao, Vinay Damodar, Uma Iyer,
Anuradha Gupta, Tulsi Nambiar, Juhi Arya, Swati Verma,
Darshana Sontakke, Authorneelima, Awantika Gupta,
Crrystal Agravat, Charvi Jain, Kirti S. Wadhwa, Niyati Singh,
Pernel, Karen, Vaishnavi S., Ridima Vaidya, Limakshi Devi,
Bhumika Kukreja

CONTENTS

Articles

MEET THE EDITOR

Sonali Sharma belongs to the hilly state of Uttarakhand. She is a postgraduate in environmental studies from Panjab University, Chandigarh. She is an aspiring researcher, a published poet, and a writer. Her poems have appeared in various anthologies and online platforms such as the Indian Periodical, Indian Ruminations, Indus Woman Writing, International Human Rights Art Festival (NY), Kali Project: Indian Women's Voices, Femasia, Setu, and Our Poetry Archive. She is the winner of India's Youngest Poet 2021 contest, organized by the Indian Film House, Bangalore. She also expresses her views on environmental concerns in Down to Earth and Indian Policy Review. Apart from her writing and research interests, she has been actively engaged with grassroots organizations working for minority needs.

ACKNOWLEDGEMENTS

An anthology, according to the Greeks, is a collection of blossoming flowers. It is true that collaboration is necessary to produce an anthology. It is not easy to walk down this path in search of blossoms that stand out above the others. Twenty-four talented and aspiring short story authors, novelists, poets, and researchers' diverse works require collaboration, patience, good humour, a lot of thought, and a persistent urge to turn pages.

The anthology's co-authors all sincerely gave their time, intellect, and strong ideas to create something inspirational. They have made every effort to adhere to the requirements and timelines necessary to ensure that this book consistently displays high quality.

Thank you to Akhila Mohan CG, Anuradha Gupta, Aruna Parandhama, Authorneelima, Awantika Gupta, Bhumika Kukreja, Charvi Jain, Crrystal Agravat, Darshana Sontakke, Dr Janki Mistry, Irene Munyiri, Juhi Arya, Karen, Kirti S. Wadhwa, Limakshi Devi, Pernel, Ridima Vaidya, Swati Verma, Tulsi Nambiar, Uma Iyer, V. Rashmi Rao, Vaishnavi. S, Vinay Damodar, and Niyati Singh for their priceless contributions towards the anthology.

I owe Ms Uma Bokil a debt of gratitude for her wise counsel, which assisted me in curating and editing this anthology. I would especially like to thank the Inkfeathers crew for their flawless printing of this anthology.

A special thank you to Mrs Rekha Pundir, Secretary, Panchayati Rule and Gender Awareness Training Institute (PRAGATI),

Dehradun, for planting the concept for this anthology in my head in the first place.

PREFACE

We can't win in shackles; breaking them will be a new day.

This anthology stems partly from the premises of my office and partly from my own thinking and a book. It was a general interaction with Mrs Rekha Pundir, Secretary, Panchayati Rule and Gender Awareness Training Institute (PRAGATI), Dehradun, about the darker side of society. With her good hold over the grassroots communities, she told me about numerous problems being faced by men and women from marginalized sections of our society. Unfortunately, their issues remain hidden, as the majority of them lack support and the courage to break the rigid shackles that bind them. I was pretty fascinated by this discussion, which I thought should be written down. At the same time, I decided to add other broader and more reflective elements to the above-mentioned discussion. Society, I believe, is a larger word and world. It has various individuals, genders, classes, castes, nationalities, issues, standards, and norms. All of it is a matter of discussion. And not just discussion, I reasoned the following week while reading a book called Social Policy: Themes and Approaches by Paul Spicker. The solutions humanity needs come in the form of responding to social problems. And the idea for the anthology was now finally complete.

The title of this anthology, "Fall to Pieces: Stand, Break, and Rise", was inspired by the word "glass". When you break a glass, it falls to pieces. The glass is analogous to the false conventions of the real world. Conventions that have no relevance in today's time. But continue to exist because of undue investments by weak and ignorant people. Such conventional glasses, which are themselves stained and occupy a shelf at the forefront of society, must be broken. New thinking and change should prevail with time. Science and logic should prevail, and humanity should win. Only when we do this do we stand in our entirety and rise above what is feeble yet made powerful.

It was a huge challenge to seek out people with stark opinions on social issues. For the anthology, I required not one or two but many such thinkers. I eventually started approaching people on social media platforms, telling them about the idea behind this book project. Thank heavens! I could reach out to an ample number of people who were curious to write for the anthology. These outstanding personalities who held a single-minded belief in this anthology come from different parts of the country. The co-authors of the book actually discuss the evils they have faced or seen someone else face. Many of them also have intentions to break such standards they dislike in the near future. All in all, these inspiring people have out-of-the-box perspectives.

In this anthology, readers may find men, women, and children sharing their stories of breaking real-life stereotypes. There are female characters in the book who have made bold decisions about their choices of motherhood and divorce. There are still other women who have come out of abusive relationships, choosing independence and a happier future for their children. Young people who have achieved their dreams despite rejection from their families and society. 'Don't eat this; don't eat that, for you may look fat!' 'Don't wear a nightgown in daylight!' 'Marry a man with a tag!' The book has many such examples that fall under the category of conventional beliefs. But what the writers have to offer comes as part and parcel of modern-day logical answers. The encounters remain as follows: 'I will eat whatever I like; fat or slim are no words to me.' 'Dress choice doesn't define me.'

'I will marry a man who loves me.' And it is not just about the stereotypes related to women and children. Men also come into the scene very neatly. Reports of women and girls being abused are quite common. But how many of us would not laugh at this episode of male abuse? In the story "Wandering About a Scandalized Road", this sensitive issue has been brought into the limelight. The taboos attached to mental illness in our society leave many affected people vulnerable. While society may declare these people useless and a burden, there are courageous people and non-governmental organizations with marked potential to change this outlook through their "Little Acts of Hope".

The section in the anthology dedicated to practical and analytical articles discusses overcoming irrational notions. For instance, a command over the English language is considered a measure of success, older men falling in love with younger women are called paedophiles, a menstruating woman is impure, LGBTQ+ people are mentally unstable, and there are superstitions attached to death. The concepts of differentiating between people based on their caste, region, or choice of inter-caste marriage are condemnable and must be reformed. The issue of postpartum depression, common among pregnant women and treated as normal because of general unawareness, has been written about in detail.

To capture the essence of their work, the co-authors of the anthology have also added personal messages at the end of their story or article. While this will help summarize their beautifully described ideas, it will also connect the readers with their thought processes. A wonderful takeaway, for sure!

In the end, it is my fervent wish that this anthology will instill a changemaker's perception in the readers. By encouraging the readers to think critically about social issues, the anthology will help them understand the difference between a false and an actual society. I have tried to incorporate stories and articles that address substantive issues at any level. Thus, my efforts throughout have been to make people question and conquer what seems like an unprogressive and stagnant belief, ritual, and norm in our world.

STORIES

DAUGHTER OF THE EARTH

Aruna Parandhama

I looked in the mirror and smiled, for I had come a long way. An academic, a writer, and an environmental activist were the various roles that defined me. No sooner did I remember how numerous forces were at play, albeit unwittingly, to make me walk backwards than my smile faded. My research on "Eco Junk and Mindfulness" was enlisted for the societally not-so-covetous "Earth Shot Prize", but to me, it meant the world just to be nominated. My ever-so-supportive spouse gave me his signature peer over my shoulder, wearing his indelible smile. 'Take care of this girl in the mirror,' he said.

Time seemed to dig its heels every time I visited my in-laws' house once a week. *Athe* (mother-in-law) noticed the emerging bald patch on her beloved son's head. 'You said you would be taking care of it?' she asked, ever so worried. This was enough to keep the news of the nomination under wraps. The family excitedly discussed the celebratory lunch. *Athe* was hosting the extended family on our tenth marriage anniversary. All the preposterous expectations from *Athe* were taken in stride; there was always a bigger fish to fry. I led the cleanliness drive in the garbage dump yards of the eastern zone as part of the volunteers' initiative of the NGO *Hasiru Dala* (Green Team). There were things to be taken care of that needed more attention than my spouse's hair care routine.

That week's get-together was largely pleasant since the focus was on planning the anniversary lunch. There was always a sense of trepidation whenever I visited my in-laws over the past few months. *Athe* had begun to coax me, 'Make a baby soon.' The first time I was told about this is vivid in my memory. These advisories were spewed with milk and honey and were always doled out clandestinely during her son's absences. I felt the old lady's motherly hankering to have someone to play with, become a grandparent, and grow the family line. With every request, the strain of desperation grew. Being a woman, I always thought I was a mother, even before physically conceiving a child. 'Isn't that true for every woman?' I wondered. I also kept close to my heart the universal mother's concern, who selflessly nurtures life. No one would understand that. I knew better.

When I returned home that evening, I had to catch up with the news about the Conference of the Parties (COP 27). "Humanity has a choice: cooperate or perish." 'It is either a climate solidarity pact or a collective suicide pact,' Antonio Guterres, Chief of the United Nations, was heard saying on the BBC at the COP27 event. The topic of the baby faded into the din of my mind. Before calling it a day, I worked on my article, "Eco Junk: Does Buying Equate to Mindfulness"? I fell asleep soon after. I woke up in a cold sweat, panting for breath, and desperately reached for the nebulizer and pumped it into my choking mouth. My spouse helped me through my anxiety bouts since I had been diagnosed with the rarest form of anxiety known in the modern world: solastalgia. Anxiety attacks in women are also synonyms for mental illness among women in India. It was my spouse's idea to keep this distress under wraps.

The first time I had an attack was right after my first cleanliness drive. Trudging through copious amounts of garbage, reeking and putrid multi-colour piles of refuse, I thought, 'How difficult it is for people to separate their waste?' 'What would it take for every person to act mindfully at least once a day?' I wondered. Poverty and lack of awareness were to blame! It was a systemic failure to not integrate our planet's concerns into the nation's pulse! The stench became worse, bordering on unbearable levels of stress. The utter monstrosity of human beings was spread out in a blanket of unmindful, unsegmented, blended waste. It was as real as the ground beneath my feet. The sheer inhumanity of what lay ahead made my veins throb in my temple. My breath felt trapped in my throat just as I was about to finish. Since that day, my nebulizer has become a staple in my sling bag.

I had enjoyed the ten years of marriage with my loving spouse, a man of few words, yet a mama's boy. The celebratory anniversary lunch was hosted by her in-laws. It was expected that they go early, so she could readily take on the role of a sous-chef and prepare a three-course meal. A few other uncles and aunts from the extended family were invited, and with them came their unsolicited advisories. Lunch was served, but the elephant in the room sat and stared at all of us. I felt like it was going to blare its trumpet at me until my ears exploded.

Refreshing *Kosambiri* salad was served, but with the unsavoury remarks of guest appearance making uncles, it felt unsettling on my palate. One aunty said, 'So, when is the good news?' I was about to remind her that the marriage anniversary was good enough news when another loose cannon aunt fired, 'It is time to make a baby. A profession is not as fulfilling as experiencing motherhood.' Another uncle said, 'The biological clock is ticking, yet you only hear the ticking of your career clock. The right things must happen at the right time.' The grandfather said, 'I am in the autumn of my life. How nice it will be to play with someone! What are you waiting for? While your in-laws still have the gift of mobility, make a baby.'

The events of the lunch thus far bore the semblance of anarchy. Amidst those motormouths, there was no mutual toleration, no self-restraint—the very anchors of democracy. Besides the cornucopia of the main course—steaming ghee rice and chicken *saaru* (curry), bitter unsolicited advisories rolled in too. The main course was also served with an imaginary take on how lonely life would get in the near future.

Yes, I would be lonely, but no one knew that our collective fate was the same, especially when the apocalypse was waiting at our doorsteps. Lao Tzu's quote, "Anything is everything, everything is nothing", reassuringly flitted through my mind. I reminded myself that life was to be lived in moments that mattered. I wanted my work to make the moments I breathed count.

At every lunch party hosted by *Athe*, her dessert always had the reputation of stealing the show. However, that day, the piping hot payasam felt the same as the scathing molten lava of a volcano that had just erupted. 'You don't seem to stop with this studying business of yours! Haven't you heard about our neighbour, the mad scientist? He kept studying all his life and look where he ended up!' The guests intended to take me on a world tour. That afternoon, we went everywhere, making detours and pit stops at Honour, Duty, and finally the twin cities of Culture and Tradition for an ordinary Indian woman. All of them were custodians of culture and pesky preachers that day.

I wondered why no one evaluated if our mother could handle more people, as she now stands on the verge of a tipping point! I experienced two tipping points that day: One as a daughter of the earth, helpless yet hopeful; another as a woman who was pushed to be ignorant and indifferent. My pulse rose, and my breath seemed rushed yet constrained. Beads of sweat copiously crowded my forehead and nape; after that, a black void took control of me. No voices were heard, only a vision. Why was I in a dark room? It felt like I was in a well. Like a cinematic display, images and thoughts merged into a pantomime, and a story played out in front of me.

There were many frogs, some with gold-rimmed glasses, and one with a walking stick. I asked them to open their eyes. They chose to keep their eyes closed. Would it be fair to the child if I decided to give birth in a world with perniciously depleted nutrition levels? I felt crippled. Two streams of light beckoned me to follow them. I wanted to pursue it as it made its way into the well. I climbed up, wishing to be accompanied, but to no avail. The frogs seemed to sit smugly in their decorated well.

The streams of light were blinding, and I followed one of the streams. Images of the Russia-Ukraine war, glaciers bursting into smithereens, oil spills, pandemics, swathes of garbage dump yards, and animals going extinct kaleidoscopically emerged and disappeared in a loop. Had the apocalypse arrived? An excruciating pain surged in and out of my veins. Sweat, fatigue, and breathlessness ensued, but the frogs stayed indifferent and smug. In the hollow blackness of the well, I felt an inexorable estrangement from the frogs. I had a choice: to return to the well and blend in with the frogs, or to walk through the swathes of garbage, attempting and failing to clean it up, to watch the animals on the verge of extinction while sounding the alarm for a better world. How do I navigate the inevitable, interminable estrangement? I have disliked open-ended questions ever since school.

I followed the light for longer than expected. With one peek inside the well, somehow, the frogs seemed to have multiplied. New frogs seemed to have joined the crowd. All of them tried to pull me back with howls and wails. Their wails faded into the sound of human voices again. I felt the thump of a defibrillator, and the human voices seemed more apparent. Silence again. I felt my spouse holding my hand when I opened my eyes after what seemed like a lifetime. Tears welled up in his eyes, yet he was wearing a smile, a combination I had not thus far seen in him.

White walls and the smell of hospital disinfectants stung my numbed senses, prodding me back to the reality of the present. However hard-hitting, it was not unwelcoming like the well. The nurse summoned the doctor soon after. Apparently, solastalgia got the better of me. This was also responsible for teleporting me into the blackness of the well. Besides medication, I was advised to complete bed rest, yoga, and counselling therapies. My spouse said he had already called *Hasiru Dala* and informed them to arrange for someone to hold the fort for me and go on with the cleanliness drive.

Curious hospital visits followed in the next week. The questions of concern implied the compulsive need to know if a heart attack begets sterility. It didn't matter. I had confided in my spouse about the well, the gory and dystopian kaleidoscope of images playing on a loop. He took me to the mirror and gently hugged me from behind. He said, 'Look at the mirror. Take care of the girl you see. You are a daughter of the earth. Straighten that crown of yours and listen to your heart. Do you have to give birth to feel like a mother? Aren't you already one by wanting to make this world a better place?'

All the scattered pieces of the jigsaw puzzle of my life seemed to rearrange themselves. The words "I am the daughter of the earth" lingered in my mind and heart. They were there to stay. As a daughter of the earth, I had to be a prisoner of hope. If and when my spouse and I conceive, the world will be a better place to live, and faith can move mountains. Until that moment, my work would carry on. My commitment to Mother Earth was more than my family's urge for a child to further the family line.

The doctor visited me dutifully. After the discharge, we held off on the weekly visits to the in-laws indefinitely. Phone catchups seemed pleasant because they were precise. Somewhere between the hospital visits and the phone catchups, the results of the much-coveted award were announced. I received a grant of one billion pounds for being adjudged the best research project under the independent research category.

Athe learned to answer the other curious extended family members in a manner she deemed fit; there were no inquiries about that. Her understanding of the *Purusha* and *Prakriti* came full circle, with some new perspectives and better sense seeming to have prevailed. She may have realized that conservation weighs more than reproduction, or she may have made peace with it. I will never know. There is always a bigger fish to fry! The second stream of light in the well showed me another series of images of the land of estrangement.

Such a calm place! Sometimes it had glass walls, and sometimes it would indefinitely turn opaque. All the frogs curiously peered every now and then to see what I was up to. I had made the choice of which light I wanted to follow. My therapies were scheduled weekly, and I had been recovering well. We spoke to our doctor about a specific medical arrangement my spouse and I had been reading about. It was time for us to go home and start afresh with more clarity and less anxiety. A fortnight after the attack, we packed our bags, and the three of us—my spouse, me, and my frozen egg—drove back home, hoping for a better world. After all, we didn't have anything to lose.

*****

Author's Message

With climate change making irreversible changes to our planet, we all find ourselves bearing the brunt of the Anthropocene. Out of all people, most women in the childbearing age suffer from solastalgia, a condition that causes distress and is produced by environmental changes. It impacts people while they are directly connected to domestic matters. The proven bleak future of our planet is making women decide not to take on motherhood. The protagonist of this story has no name since strains of it could be each of our stories with varying intensities. Each of us born on this planet are sons and daughters of the Earth. To serve this great Mother is equivalent to motherhood for me and those like me. One doesn't become a mother just by making a child, but also by nurturing what is around you, evaluating if this planet is ready for more of our species, and acting on the truth that is prompted by our selfless conscience.

2

A LIFE NOT BY CHOICE

Limakshi Devi

After I looked up from my laptop screen at that hour of the morning, I could not help but close my eyes as they burned from working on the screen all night. And when I opened them slowly, I saw someone. At first, it felt like an illusion. But gradually I could recognize the face—it was Mom's. There she was sipping her cup of tea, lost in her thoughts. I wanted to go and kiss her forehead, wishing her a good morning, but something stopped me, something from within, and all I could do was watch.

I kept staring at that face; I could now look better, and I noticed how time had taken its toll on her: the wrinkles that spoke of her worries over the years, the dark circles that spoke of her sleepless nights, and the half-grey hair strands that spoke of how unconcerned she had become about her appearance. All I could see in that dimly lit room was that face, and how that face was the answer to all my questions. Her face could calm all my restless nerves. But today, that face scared me. And then suddenly, she looked at me, and we kept staring at each other until that familiar face was no longer familiar to me. The face that I had known for years was turning into an unfamiliar one.

I turned cold when I figured out what was happening. I was now struggling to breathe, so I rushed to the window to open it and get a touch of reality and not my imagination. The cold air touched my face now, but was this the touch of reality or just a band-aid that hides the wound but does not cure it? I recognized the woman I saw today as not being my mother. Mom was miles away from me. We just spoke on the phone a few hours ago. This face that I was staring at a few minutes ago was mine; it was me years from now. It was the reality that was more real than the gust of wind.

My life was constantly going through a rare pandemonium, escaping from which would give me immense euphoria. It was the emptiness that was now taking control of my mind. It seems too hard and too endless to bear such hollowness, so you reach for a cigarette, the phone, or the novel lying next, all in an attempt to escape this hollowness. But the question is, until when?

My relationship with my mom while growing up had always been special and different. And now the euphoria really made sense. My fears were staring into my eyes a few minutes ago, and all I could do was stare back and do nothing. I had always tried to bridge the gap between life and living for Mom, for she meant the world to me. She has said a million times that I am her world. For some, they might just be words. For my mom, that was the truth. This woman made me her sun, and so her world revolved around me.

Father left us when I was a child, too young to remember how he made the house feel. Growing up, I always knew it was my mother and me against the world, which constantly tried to feed her with thoughts that it was her fault that our father left us and that she would raise me in the same way—incapable of ever keeping a man.

I was suddenly disrupted by the notification tone of my phone. I saw from my notification window that it was a text from the clinic that my reports were ready to be collected. I did not dare to open the text and dismissed it from the notification window. Gradually, reality began to take shape, and I rushed to get ready for the day. How do you get ready for the day? By putting on new clothes but carrying the same stale thoughts you've been carrying around for weeks? By hiding your dark circles and your cigarette burnt lips with makeup? I guess we all do wear masks every day.

I arrived at my parking spot and paused to gather myself to appear in front of my colleagues. The security guard, like always, wished me a warm good morning, but all I could gather from him today was a faint smile. Was this a good morning? Well, I have had better ones, and I guessed he could figure it out just by looking at me. While pretending to look at my phone and heading for the elevator, I avoided making direct eye contact with anyone nearby. I shoved my phone in my pocket when I reached the elevator, and just then I heard a familiar message tone. I had a custom notification tone set for him to ensure I never missed a text as and when it reached me. He who? Just one of the men I couldn't keep, but the only one I could honestly say I loved with everything I had.

I hesitated to look at the text but opened it anyway.

'I request you to delete the pictures of us; it was a mistake, and I do not want any of it coming back to haunt me ever,' it read.

Mistake? I was a mistake? We were a mistake? Why does one not realize when they are making a mistake but so proudly call it one later and move on? He kept calling it a relationship while promising a future but proved it to be nothing but an affair today by calling it a mistake.

Yes, he was married the whole time but complained about how badly he wanted to get out of the marriage. And that he would talk soon with his wife and end it, as he said he had never been sure about anything in his life more than us. Was that a mistake?

I was stopped and forced to get out of my train of thoughts by a colleague who got into the elevator on the eighth floor. We had a town hall in an hour, and I just spent the whole night on the presentation, which I was not even sure I was ready to present. I walked to my manager and told him how I felt; I could not be the presenter today, but he would not listen to a word I had to say about it. I agreed halfheartedly.

'You've got to work when you've got to work, right? Work-life balance, they all say.'

They have had arguments about why women cannot rise in workplaces, and that is because they think with their hearts and not their heads. I owe this to all the women out there, and especially to my mother, who had never let her personal life interfere with her professional one. In fact, for years she forgot she had a personal life; it was during the last years of her work tenure that she realized her work never paid her enough for all the hard work and sacrifices she made.

I gave the presentation and accepted the appreciation while constantly thinking about the doctor's appointment. I guessed I was not all about the work-life balance. Suddenly I felt weak on my knees, and everything blurred out; one moment I was faking a smile, and the next I was blank. I collapsed on the floor and was rushed to the medic's room. I regained my senses and confessed that I hadn't had the chance to eat since yesterday. My manager decided to give me the rest of the day off. I rested for a while and returned to my car.

I made a few phone calls and moved my appointment.

The doctor was not there yet, but I would be the first one she would see once she arrived, they said. So, I sat there, waiting for my name to be called. A couple came and sat next to me; she looked like she was in her third trimester. They looked like a happy couple, whatever that means. We looked happy too; we had our moments too, but is it always what it looks like? Is it?

The doctor arrived, and the clinic staff handed me my report and escorted me to the chamber. I sat where I was asked to, and the doctor gave me a smile.

'How are you today, dear? You look pale.'

I smiled and handed her the reports. I did not dare open the reports until then.

'Well, the report shows a gestational sac, but it is still too early to detect any dating scan,' Doctor Kaur said after looking over the reports.

I suddenly forgot how to speak—or breathe, for that matter. Everything looked like a lie, yet everything was the truth. I was left by a man who was talking about abandoning his marriage and kid, and here I was told that I had conceived his child. Who wouldn't want another pair of those brown eyes, another set of those infectiously smiling lips, or that perfect carved nose? I did; I always did, and today I was not even sure.

'Oh, dear, you know there are options for terminating it in case that's what you decide,' she added, reading my face and interrupting my thoughts.

But I went back to my thoughts again. Just the day before, when I came in for an ultrasound, I was given a very horrid look by the woman who was doing my ultrasound when I told her I wasn't married. Is that what I wanted? That horrid look forever?

I was interrogated my entire life when my father did not show up in the PTMs or to see me perform on sports day or annual day. I was given that horrid look all my life when I said my father did not live with us, but I immediately had to add that he went on a business trip after witnessing that look. It was a business trip sometimes and a leg injury on others, but he was never there. Did I want to be questioned for the rest of my life about who the father of my child was? Would I be spending my life answering why a father was missing in the scenarios that involved me throughout my life?

Moreover, if I decided to keep the child, did I want my child to live the same life I had lived? Covering up for an absent father, learning how to make lies, watching other kids have their father around, and wishing that a fairy appeared to rewrite the story and magically make the father appear?

'I want to discuss termination,' I finally said.

'Sure, since the pregnancy is still in its early stages, we can get it terminated through medications. There is no need for any other procedure to be involved here unless the medications do not work. We will have a follow-up USG to check that as soon as possible. But in cases like yours, the tablets are sufficient,' she said, before beginning to write the prescription.

She pushed the prescription towards me while explaining how I needed to take the medications and not work during the course of the medication. After she was done, she gave me a smile to indicate that her consultation was done.

I took the prescription and got up to leave. How easy it would have been for her to simply write the prescription and get rid of me! She would go home just like any other day. Why shouldn't she? After all, it was a regular day for us. It was I who was having the day of my life.

I got out of the clinic and decided to call Mom; I had missed two of her calls already. I needed her, and I needed her the most. So, I sat in my car and decided to call her. After just two rings, she picked up and complained that I ignored her all day. I opened my mouth to tell her I was busy, but all I could muster was that I felt sorry, and then I started crying.

I knew she felt the most helpless when I cried, and under no circumstance could I tell her about the pregnancy. She would be devastated. She would blame herself for things that were not her fault at all. I should have known better. I should have known better.

I told her I was just having a bad day at work, and she told me how it was part of the package: 'You can be a mountaineer your whole life, but it is not possible to climb every mountain that you set your foot on,' she said. She had an answer for everything. My encyclopaedia, I'd always say, even though I was constantly correcting her facts.

I went home and decided to eat, so I made myself some scrambled eggs. Turned on the TV but decided to leave it on the home screen. I took my phone and read his text again: 'It was a mistake, and I did not want any of it coming back to haunt me ever.'

Sure, I contemplated letting him know, but reading his text made me sure that I did not want to fall weak in front of him ever again. I decided to start the medicine and took the pill. The process had started; there was no going back, and in just three days I got rid of everything that belonged to him.

I curled up on the sofa, remembering all the things he said but never meant. I remembered waking up at 3 a.m. with my limbs wrapped in a tangled sheet, next to a man who slept beside me, clearly disturbed by clearly disturbing thoughts. Maybe he was dreaming a bad dream, and I left the sheet and wrapped myself around him, and suddenly, he looked relaxed and peaceful for a quick glance.

I wished that for myself today. I wished he would be here to wrap me in his arms and tell me that everything would be alright. I thought that's all we really want—someone to look after us when our walls are down, and our bodies are bare. But most of all, we need a saviour. My mom, while making me the sun of her ever-revolving world, made me the saviour of her life; my problems were always bigger than hers, and my sadness was always greater.

Now the question that really haunts me is, 'Does the saviour have a saviour of his own?'

*****

Author's Message

Women are said to be God's favourite because they have been granted the gift of bringing a life onto this Earth. But often, a blessing can turn into a curse. Women are born with the biggest responsibility on this Earth—to decide whether the environment around them and they themselves can nurture a life to maturity. But society should be willing to grant every woman the choice to be a mother, a giver, and an eternal care provider.

3

THE BURDEN OF A SOLITAIRE

Kirti S Wadhwa

Jyoti was weeping softly, sitting at the foot of the bed. Light from the bathroom door was escaping and giving off a dim lighting effect. Wearing a yellow-coloured cotton salwar kameez, she was pressing her right forearm. Her body had bruises and marks. In the next room were her kids, sitting quietly on the blue velvet sofa. They didn't know how to comfort Ma. She got up, opened the side drawer of the bed, and started looking for a painkiller. She had no idea what she had done and therefore couldn't understand how to fix it. All she was told was that she deserved it.

This is the story of the Arora family, a so-called upper-middle-class family living in a posh area of South Delhi. Jyoti and Rajesh had been married for fifteen years. The residence was a huge five-bedroom apartment, and this scenario was like a weekly show. Her in-laws adopted the "carrots and sticks" policy to ensure that Jyoti's mental volcano doesn't burst. She was praised for having handled the most notorious man in the family with such poise. Why would they address the fact that domestic violence is a crime? The repercussions could be devastating! Henceforth, she was indoctrinated with the Devi Sita image.

Jyoti was the daughter of an army officer. Raised in a liberal-minded middle-class family with lots of love and care abound, Jyoti was a confident and cheerful girl. With a fair skin tone, a medium build, a curvaceous body, and black wavy waist-length hair, she was conventionally attractive. At twenty-three, she found a tall, dark, handsome, well-built man with curly hair very appealing. Being a self-made alpha male, he was worshipped by society as a "success". His drive to get things done was attention-grabbing. Predictably enough, her female instinct chose him. Rajesh lived with his mother, an elder brother, and his wife.

After getting married in November 1993, Jyoti's life took a roller-coaster-like turn. Domestic violence started after one month of the honeymoon period. In the beginning, it was mental; maybe he was testing the waters. Episodes like throwing her clothes from the closet, not having dinner dates, making her do all household work single-handedly, etc. were common. What would be his answer if questioned? Your father did not provide an adequate dowry. I am ashamed in front of society. Jyoti's marks and bruises themselves told the scenario to her parents, and henceforth they suggested Jyoti leave him since greed knows no limits. Now, Jyoti was standing at a crossroads—either with her parents or in-laws? That's when she thought of a risky middle ground. She will give Rajesh a child that will keep him calm and happy, and then she will apologize to her parents. As a result, she chose to isolate herself from her parents as a temporary solution.

In 1994, a year after her marriage, a daughter was born. The family named her Karishma. Everyone praised her white-pink skin and curly hair. The fresh apple of Arora's family, with her small hands and her curling toes, mesmerized everyone. But things started going south swiftly for Jyoti. Rajesh's mind started working: she has a baby, and her father is a middle-class retired army man. Even if her parents forgive her, how will an old man handle the societal and financial burden of a divorced daughter and a granddaughter? The result was that he had a free hand to physically abuse Jyoti. She was beaten up for petty reasons like less salt, a dirty towel, or just anything. Jyoti was not allowed to use the washing machine, watch TV, or use the landline telephone.

Before going to bed, Rajesh used to give Jyoti a time slot to wash the clothes, usually from 5 a.m. to 7 a.m. Rajesh and the sister-in-law didn't stop there; if the bed sheet was warm, it meant she was resting during the day, for which she was beaten up. It was a real struggle since new-borns do not sleep at night. Whenever the daughter slept, Jyoti rushed into the kitchen. After all, a man on an empty stomach could become enraged! But the kitchen was like a rocky terrain—she was not an expert cook. The 1990s had no YouTube, either. She was often taunted and mocked: *'Isko bas parantha banana ata hai woh bhi pata nahi konsi country ka map hota hai.'* ('She just knows how to make parantha; that too, we don't know which country's map it is.')

Nevertheless, Rajesh had devised a successful formula for keeping a sex slave with minimum maintenance. Henceforth, Jyoti gave birth to a son in 1995, another one in 1996, and then another son in 1999.

The tables turned, and a boon was given to her under the façade of a bane. It was August 25th, 1999, and at 3:15 am, the doorbell rang. Rajesh got up, walked through the dark hallway barefoot, with messy hair, yawning, and unlocked the wooden door. An aluminium door stood next to the wooden door. Rajesh saw around eight to nine men in formal shirts and pants standing with straight faces. With them were three to four policemen. Rajesh's eyes were wide open. Who the hell are these people? Collecting himself in a jiffy, with extreme humility and politeness, he asked, 'Yes, sir, what do you want?' At the front, ostensibly leading the group was a middle-aged man wearing spectacles who was half bald and built like a hulk.

Rajesh said, 'It's an income tax raid.' 'Open the door.' 'Sir, but we are....' said Rajesh. The officer interrupted, 'If you do not open the door, we will have to break in; decide now.' Rajesh opened the door. All the family members shifted into a room; the adults were in shock, and the children were sleepy. Jyoti arranged four bed sheets on the floor next to the bed on which the children could sleep; all she cared about was their next day's school. The IT department turned the whole house upside down—mattresses were torn, things in the almirahs were scattered on the floor, walls were being checked through hard knocking to see if they were hollow, and cars' seats were torn and thoroughly checked. The cash was discovered by the IT department; Rajesh and Anil were arrested, and the females and children were ordered not to leave the house until permission was granted. They then called a friend, who let them go by paying more than the penalty amount. After that, they realized that a Special Investigation Team (SIT) had been constituted for such businessmen. They decided to uproot the problem forever. A friend suggested that they should open a retail shop for female garments. But they didn't have the skill set for it. This was when her sister-in-law Anita realized that Jyoti had a diploma in fashion design.

Foreseeably enough, Jyoti was asked to go run the shop. She had the foresight to open a female clothing store. The shop was a ground-floor shop in the middle of the local market. Despite the huge competition, profits started pouring in soon. Jyoti's life changed overnight! She didn't do any household work; there was a full-time maid just to look after her kids. She was certainly enjoying the whole process. Rajesh also stopped abusing her physically or mentally. But he did send her a clear message: 'Better stay subservient; else your wings will be clipped.'

There was another reason for Rajesh's changed behaviour. The elder brother's wife, Anu, had left because of domestic violence. Anu was Anil's second wife. The first wife had taken a divorce on the same grounds. Anu went back to her maternal home and filed a divorce case. The Arora brothers then realized that hitting female members of the family would cost them a lot in terms of social prestige and money. So, Rajesh's family asked him to stop beating Jyoti, or else she could mirror Anu's steps.

This went on from 1999 to 2006. Rajesh and Jyoti had been married for twelve years at this point. He was busy at the shop, and she was juggling between the shop and her kids. Jyoti's new normal was expensive clothes, diamonds, and brands. She hid all this from her husband, or else he would say, *'Tere baap ke ghar se aya hai kya?'* ('Has it come from your father's house?') But she was never really rewarded for her hard work and acumen. No anniversary, no birthday celebrations, nothing! She was like a single mom who worked and then went back to her kids. The only difference was that she had the burden of a solitaire on her finger, so no man from outside dared look at her as a predator. But did that come without a price? No, she was always kept under pressure. But Jyoti was happy since her kids were being brought up in the best of ways. They went to the best school and had the best tuition and extracurricular activities—exactly what she lacked as a child. In the same span of seven years, both Anil and Rajesh learned from Jyoti the skill set of running a female garment business.

In 2007, Jyoti was working in a corner of the shop, and Rajesh was at the cash counter. As her brow furrowed, she noticed Rajesh smiling and stroking a woman's hand. *'Idhar aa, Mukesh,'* ('Come here Mukesh') she said to her favourite salesman, and Mukesh dashed over with the question, *'Ji Bhabhi batao?'* ('Yes, sister-in-law tell me?') Jyoti, in a demanding voice, asked, *'Ye ladki kon hai?'* ('Who is this girl?') Mukesh turned towards the floor and went mute. She, with a straight face, said, *'Kitni ladkiyan hai?'* ('How many girls are there?') Mukesh said, *'Kyu fasa rahe ho bhabhi me naukar aadmi hu.'* ('Sister-in-law, please don't get me into this; I am a mere servant.')

She went to the chair next to the trial rooms, took out her purple Gucci purse from the white fur coat she was wearing that day, took out ten notes of five hundred rupees each, and gave them to Mukesh. *'Yele, tere pure month ka incentive, is week ke end tak mujhe har ladki ki pehchan chahiye,'* she explained. ('Take this; this is your entire month's incentive; by this weekend I want the identities of all the girls.') Mukesh agreed. She stopped coming to the shop at the same time to give Rajesh a free hand.

Next week, the salesmen confirmed her doubt and pointed out the females Rajesh may have had an affair with—customers and salesgirls. Now Jyoti wanted proof; she could not make allegations against Rajesh just on the word of a salesman. Moreover, that poor chap could lose his job. She told the salesman to give her a signal whenever any of his probable girlfriends entered the shop. A woman entered the shop, and Mukesh signalled Jyoti. She was fair-skinned, obese, and short; her blonde hair was half tied with a cherry-red clip. She was wearing a cherry-red A-line dress that reached her knees. Her four-inch heel made her appear to be about 5.5 inches tall. Jyoti switched on the video camera of her phone and hid it behind her dupatta, focusing the camera on Rajesh's face. The camera recorded Rajesh giving her his business card. The female took it and smiled at him. He started the same stroking, gently feeling her skin, and then left. It was the first night in the Arora house when a wife raised her voice.

She fought, screamed, and asked questions! Jyoti had always thought that her husband had a bad temper, but he was loyal to her. This hurt her more than the physical beating. She felt like the stupidest person in the world, an illusion she had lived in for twelve years. Rajesh said, 'Lord Krishna used to do raasleela; every man does it.' Jyoti, though depressed, continued to showcase her anger. She started insulting him openly at the shop in front of the salespeople. She laid off all the salesgirls but could not stop the customers. Upon confrontation, she realized they were prostitutes and had been in touch with Rajesh for a long time. They never paid the bill for anything. After strictly interrogating one, she found out that they were given lots of expensive gifts on birthdays, festivals, etc. This was like molten lava in her ears! She wasn't allowed to buy a piece of clothing from the business that she worked so hard for, and these women were being given expensive gifts in exchange for rubbing their bodies with her husband!

On the other hand, Rajesh had now started thinking about what to do. Anil and Rajesh made a plan. Rajesh paid three of his favourite salesmen, Imra, Chotu, and Yadav, to confront Jyoti whenever he was around. After a few days, Jyoti was helping change the display, and those three salesmen went to Jyoti and said, *Bhabhi agar yai karna hai to hm dukan pr kaam nahi karenge.* ('Sister-in-law, if this is what we need to do, then we will not work at the shop.') Jyoti, with an utterly confused look on her face, said, 'Kya?' ('What?') *Aap paisa chori karti ho and hum sale nahi karte,* ('You steal money, and we don't do sales.') Imran fixed his gaze on her. Jyoti said, 'What? *Paise chori?* ('What? Steal money?') How dare you make such allegations against me?' This whole scene was happening at the entrance door of the shop. Rajesh wanted to take revenge by allowing the salesmen to insult her. He then came and said, *'Jyoti tu ghar jaa, and tum teeno jaa kar apna kaam karo.'* ('Jyoti, go home, and you three go and do your work.')

'Mene video dekha hai tu paise nikal rahi thi,' ('I have seen the video; you were stealing money.') Rajesh explained that night. Jyoti explained why she would steal from her own business. But before she could give any logic, she was beaten up by a leather belt—even the neighbours could hear the "Wutussh" voice of the belt hitting her skin and her screams. Rajesh said, 'Don't you dare insult or question me ever again.' Jyoti then understood that this was an act of revenge. She was further ordered to stay at home and not interfere in the business of the shop ever again.

The kids had grown up by then. Jyoti's eldest daughter, Karishma, was fourteen, and her youngest, Jai, was nine years old. Govind, her other son, was thirteen years old, and Krishna was twelve years old. They were witnesses to everything.

So now there is a mother who has an abusive and manipulative husband and four innocent children. She is financially dependent, has no idea about her rights as a citizen, and doesn't even know where her parents are. Will she bear the burden alone forever? Will she keep on crying in a room with dim light, thinking about what she did wrong? We'll see that in the next story.

4

SHE THREW AWAY THE SOLITAIRE

Kirti S Wadhwa

The story is still stuck in dim light, but Jyoti's skin has loosened up and she has wrinkles. Her eyes speak of the pain she has been undergoing. She walks tilted, and her knees have gone weak due to continuous bashing. She isn't the same talkative person. It's 2015—years of beatings have taken a toll on her physical and mental health. Is she suffering from depression? We don't know since she never had it diagnosed.

It was September 8th, 2015, Jyoti's eldest son Govind's birthday. The kids wanted to go out to dinner with their families, but their father refused because he was tired from work. Karishma wore a bodycon baby pink dress that was knee-length, and her curly hair was in a closed bun. Govind, having the same tall, dark, and handsome look as his father, wore a royal blue shirt and black jeans. Krishna and Jai were called Jai-Veeru of Sholay; hence, they wore the same white shirt and blue jeans to look alike. Jyoti wore a maroon suit with a dark green border and a dark green satin dupatta, and she half-tied her hair. They decided to cut the cake with their father after they got back from dinner.

As soon as they opened the house's door to leave, Rajesh pulled Jyoti by her hair and dragged her to the lobby area. He started beating her with a wooden stick. He hit her kneecap so hard, she shouted,

'*Aaah bhagwan, bacha le is aadmi se,* please!' ('God, save me from this man, please!') Jyoti was already taking painkillers for her knee. This was not an uncommon sight for the children, but Karishma couldn't see her mother in such pain anymore. Suddenly she remembered what she had read on a billboard near her college: "Women's Helpline: Call 1091 for any type of abuse". From the corner of the lobby, she slipped into the washroom. Karishma's hands trembled and her eyes watered in fear. '*Hanji batao ye kya hua hai?*' ('Yes, tell me what has happened?') a woman asked. She told her that her mother was being beaten up by her father, and the woman, in the same monotonous tone, asked, '*Address bataiye, hum police bhejte hain.*' ('Tell us the address; we will send the police.') She told her the address, and the woman then disconnected the phone. Karishma's first thought—is that it?

But two seconds later, she realized that either my mother gets saved, or my father is going to beat me to death too. After four to five minutes, Karishma's phone rang. The father shouted, 'Who the hell is calling you at night? I'm going to beat you to death too now!' Before he could get hold of her, she pushed him away and ran swiftly. She opened the main door, rushed down the stairs, and then picked up the phone. '*Hanji madam, helpline par phone kia tha hum aap ke ghar ke bahar khade hain kahan ho aap,*' ('Yes, madam, you called on the helpline; we are standing outside your house; where are you?') enquired a man. She tried to open the main gate of the building, but her father was smarter than she thought. He had asked the building's guard to lock the gate from outside so that Jyoti could not run away anywhere.

Karishma started shouting, '*Gate kholo, uncle, inhone hame lock kar diya hai.*' ('Open the gate, uncle, they have locked us.') The two policemen stopped the PCR mid-way and came out following Karishma's voice. They then opened the gate. Her brothers and mother had also come outside at that time, unaware of what Karishma had done. After Karishma told her mother, Jyoti complained about what was happening. The police officer saw the blue marks on Jyoti's body and asked her to file an F.I.R. against her husband right away. *'Jab tak bleeding nahi hoti mushkil hai,'* ('Until the bleeding takes place, it is difficult.') Rajesh explained. The police said, *'Tujhe abhi bata dunga kya mushkil hai kya nahi.'* ('I will tell you right away what is difficult and what is not.') Then Rajesh politely took both officers to a corner and offered money. Probably the officers could not risk their jobs because of the evidence that the marks were fresh and visible. If they did not file a complaint, their supervisor could question them. We don't know whether they took the money, but they could not stop Jyoti from filing the complaint.

But a caveat appeared, and Jyoti's mind said, 'If I file the complaint, where will I go after that?' or 'What if he kills me if I file a complaint?' On the other hand, 'If I don't file a complaint, he will continue beating me, and I might die today.' Jyoti then filed a complaint and moved out of the house. Her kids trailed her around like mama duck. All of them checked into a nearby hotel; PCR had dropped them off there. Govind had called a friend of his to lend him some money. The hotel room was a three-star. A double bed and a brown velvet sofa set—there was not enough room to fit five people comfortably. Nonetheless, all they could think was "Now what"?

The next morning, Jyoti went to the doctor to get treated for her knee injury. The same morning, Rajesh had found out about the hotel, reached there, and paid the owner to throw them out. The hotel owner was a friend of his. On the same day, the owner ordered those five people to leave. Even if it had not been Rajesh's doing, how could they survive out in the world without any money? Those five people with long faces were returned to prison.

Now Jyoti's in-laws were scared; their pet cat had learned to use her claws. So, they opted for psychological abuse. Some new ground rules were set. Jyoti and her daughter were not allowed to go outside the house, not even to the nearby market to buy groceries, etc. Karishma would drop out of college if female mobile phones were not available. She took leave and lied at home that she had quit. While the women couldn't be touched, Rajesh and Anil started thrashing and insulting the sons. This was most likely an indirect form of blackmail directed at Jyoti; if she did not conform to their whims and wishes, her children would suffer.

The situation went beyond limits when Rajesh tried to frame his sons in a fake drug case. The three sons were given movie tickets by Rajesh. All three of them joyfully took their father's car. While they were stuck in traffic, a known policeman, who was Rajesh's friend, stopped them. He took them to the police station and asked them to write on a piece of paper, 'Two kg of heroin have been found in my car, and I take full responsibility for that.' With their phones taken away, the boys were scared. Of course, this was illegal. After collecting himself, Govind refused. The officer grabbed Govind by the collar and threatened to beat him to death if they didn't write. Govind calmly said, '*Daldo sir, likh kar to nahi dene wala. Hath lagana dur ki baat hai, hamesha ke liye to rakh nahi paoge, lock me up.*' ('Put me in, sir; I will not write. To put your hand on me is a faraway thing; you will not be able to keep me forever; lock me up.') The officer then pushed him aside and dialled a number.

Rajesh came, and he further mounted the pressure, favouring the police. 'If you think this is right, Dad, *aap likh kar sign kar do,*' ('If you think this is right, Dad, you write and sign.') they exclaimed, their eyes wide open. Why would a father do such a thing to his children? Anyway, the boys were adamant about their decision. After a few hours of daily soap opera drama, the officer had to let them go. Now, Rajesh and Anil realized that the law is not a weapon that we just lubricate with money and use as per our desires.

Furious and frustrated, the notorious Arora brothers made a new plan. This time, they would take it up a notch. They got a drug to add to Jyoti's food that would weaken her heart muscles, the result of which was that her heart would slowly stop beating. A natural death— the problem would be uprooted forever. After her death, who had the balls to file a complaint against both of them? As a result, there is no risk of a post-mortem examination. Controlling the children without the mother would be a cakewalk. The very next day, they started putting drugs in her food. But another logistical blocker appeared: she was cooking and serving the food. Plus, how do they put it just in her food and no one else's? If they added the drug to the whole dish, they would be eating it too. Here, Rajesh scripted a small drama.

He accused her of putting drugs in his food, due to which his sugar levels were dwindling. Rajesh had diabetes, so the excuse worked. He then quickly took out a portion of food from his plate and asked her to eat it to prove herself. Jyoti knew she hadn't done anything; she ate without hesitation. Rajesh didn't know the taste of the drug, but Jyoti felt a distinct taste while eating. She ignored these two to three times, but after that, she told her children about the distinct taste in the food she was forced to eat; this made the children vigilant. They would stay around when food was served to Rajesh.

One fine day, Rajesh was adding the drug to a curry, and the youngest son, Jai, saw it peeping through the washroom. He ran and told Karishma. Karishma came running and mixed the curry with the drugs for Rajesh's curry. Her furious father slapped her and said, *'Dimag hai ya nahi?'* ('Do you have brains or not?')

Jyoti came running and asked what happened. *'Aapke khaane me drugs mile rahe the, Mummy,'* ('They were putting drugs in your food, Mummy.') Karishma said. Then Jyoti and the children asked him to eat the curry. Rajesh smashed the curry bowl against the front wall. The curry spilt all over. He wanted to erase any evidence of drugs being in it. The same night, Rajesh and Anil were questioned. They shrugged off all allegations: *'Aisi bakwas karni hai to nikal jao hamare ghar se. Akal aa jayegi kuch din bahar rahoge,'* ('If this is the kind of rubbish you want to do, then get out of our house. Your mind will come to its right place if you stay outside for some days.') said Sari. By then, the mother-daughter duo had learned their legal rights, and they challenged each other to call the police. As soon as the police angle came in, they were quiet. But her health took a toll, and Jyoti's heart weakened. Her pulse would go dangerously low.

Now the drug addiction had stopped, but Rajesh and Anil couldn't be trusted. Krishna, Jyoti's third child, gave her a secret phone that she could use to contact anyone she wanted. He could not give her the phone since his father would check his call details. Jyoti thought, 'I don't know how long I will live; let me hear my mother's voice at least.'

She dialled with trembling hands. The number no longer existed; she dialled her sister Preeti's number—that too was invalid. So, then she called her closest cousin. Jyoti had written all the numbers in a diary and hidden it long ago. Her cousin told her that Rajesh used to intimidate her parents and would get their daughters raped, kidnapped, or killed. They then sold everything and moved to Australia forever. Jyoti's heart sank; her eyes watered. How would she ever be able to meet or contact them? She asked for the Australian phone number, and the cousin gave her Preeti's house number. Jyoti called that number, and a faint elderly woman's voice said, 'Hello?' Jyoti said, 'Mummy, the old lady cut the phone.' Jyoti was shocked. She sat on the bed and held her head between her hands, thinking her mother didn't want to talk to her.

The same night, the phone vibrated; it was her mother. Jyoti rushed into the washroom and picked up the phone. Preeti said, 'Hello, Jyoti.' Jyoti, trying to get some words out of her mouth, responded, *'Preeti kaisi hai tu? Mummy, papa, kaise hain?'* (Preeti, how are you? Mummy, Papa, how are you both?') Preeti said, 'Before we talk any further, I have one question.' Jyoti, puzzled, said, *'Haan bol?'* ('Yes, say?') Preeti said, 'We need to know it's you and not Rajesh's trap, so answer this: 'What was the name of our dog?' If you are not under any pressure, give the right name.' Jyoti replied, 'It was Peggy; we had him when we were kids, but why are you asking about Peggy all of a sudden and what trap?' After this, Jyoti's parents came on the phone, and all four poured their hearts out. Jyoti explained everything that had happened to her; her parents recited their side of the story.

After listening to everything, her parents decided to get Jyoti out of that hell before she died. They contacted the Delhi Commission of Women (DCW) for help. DCW then called Jyoti and asked her to visit the office and submit the complaint in writing. Her daughter, Karishma, made an excuse about buying some books. Anil asked Jyoti to accompany her if it gets dark. They reached the DCW office. The waiting area was a typical government office setting: wooden benches without paint, ceiling fans making noise, and a water cooler at the corner. Females of different strata—different age groups, rural and urban, poor and rich—were tired and waiting for their turn.

Finally, after an hour, Jyoti was called inside. It was a small room with two chairs, an almirah, a noisy air conditioner, and old light-yellow paint with black marks. A young female in an orange-yellow salwar kameez, seemingly underweight, was sitting. She asked Jyoti to write her whole story on paper. Jyoti did, and the officer then signed it and put the DCW stamp on it. The officer, though very rational, developed a respect for Jyoti's age and politely asked her what she wanted; Jyoti bluntly replied, 'Leave that hell hole forever.' A DCW officer gave her a date and said, 'You come here on this date, and we will then go to your house, where you can collect your belongings, and then we will drop you off safely wherever you want.'

Jyoti was thrilled. Karishma told her brothers about this news the same day. All four kids agreed to leave their father forever after seeing his deeds. All were thrilled; a new chapter in their lives was about to begin. Jyoti told her parents about the news, and they were elated too. But where would they go if they left? Jyoti's parents were not in Delhi, and who would be generous enough to take in a family of five grown people?

Anyway, D-day was tomorrow. This was the day that the twenty-five-yearlong bondage and slavery would end. Will Jyoti and her kids be successful in winning their freedom? Or will the bravery shown to date go in vain? Let's explore that in the next story.

5

HER BARE FINGERS ARE FREE

Kirti S Wadhwa

D-Day is November 26th, 2015

Neither Jyoti nor any of her kids had a peaceful sleep. Their lives, as they knew, were going to change forever.

The children planned that Krishna would use the pretext of his college admission, for which he would need to go to Noida, and he would need an elder's company. On this pretext, Jyoti and Krishna left at 11 a.m. The rest of the three children, under tremendous pressure, waited long and patiently on the same blue velvet sofa. Rajesh and Anil had created so much fear that the children thought they would be killed or jailed if the plan didn't work.

At 1:30 p.m., the doorbell rang. Karishma ran and opened the door. Her eyes were lit as if she had seen an angel. Jyoti and Krishna entered with a DCW female officer and a policeman. Anil was at home at that time and was in utter shock. He quickly called Rajesh and told him the scenario. After that, he started shouting and abusing Jyoti, and the police officer then threatened him to be quiet or a case would be filed against him. Jyoti and the children were meanwhile packing their stuff. They had decided that whatever they could pack in two hours would suffice. They didn't want to give Rajesh and Anil too much time to plan an escape.

After approximately an hour, Rajesh came home. He said, *'Jana hai to jao but ye samaan mere paise se ayah hai isko lekar jaoge to chori ka case laga dunga.'* ('If you want to go, then go, but these items have come from my money; if you take them, I will impose a case of theft.') They had four bags that contained some clothes for every climate in Delhi, their IDs, some crockery, and the children's course books. The children decided that they were leaving even if their father denied them their basic belongings. Anil then paid the DCW officer and the policeman to not help Jyoti or the children. The DCW woman then pressured Jyoti to sign a document stating that she was taking all her essentials with her and could not take anything else from Rajesh's house. Under that pressure, Jyoti was scummed, but she signed because this woman was her only hope for starting a new life with the essence of freedom.

After five hours of drama and verbal abuse, the mother and children left at around 6:30 p.m. It was cold and dark outside. They were in their night clothes and slippers but without any sweaters. Anil, mockingly, said to Jai, *'Yele beta five hundred rupaye, aur chahiye ho to aa kar le jaio.'* ('Son, take these five hundred rupees, and if you want more, then please come and take them.') Anil and Rajesh were confident that they wouldn't survive in this world since they had no money. Rajesh knew what he had done to Jyoti's parents, so he was pretty confident that no relative would dare take these five people. These two brothers had a lot of haughtiness in their money.

The DCW woman then dropped them off at the nearest metro station. Jyoti's mother had requested that her best friend keep Jyoti and the kids for three days as an emergency since Rajesh was only aware of the relatives and not their close friends. She was an old widow with two kids living in a two-bedroom apartment. The kind lady gave them warm clothes, food, and bedding to comfort them, all five of them in utter shock at what would happen.

On the third day, Jyoti's father arranged another accommodation for one of his best friends. The family of five was changing houses. His friend, Om, lived alone in a five-bedroom apartment in Gurgaon, where they lived for another week. Meanwhile, Jyoti went house hunting. But many obstacles were waiting here for this family.

First, they had no IDs, and generating a copy would take some time. Second, they needed a guarantor so that someone could rent their house. Third, their budget was extremely tight. Lastly, Jyoti had a young daughter, so she needed a safe neighbourhood to live in.

Also, they had no clothes, including undergarments, to change into. Jyoti's parents asked everyone they knew in Delhi to help their daughter. It was Delhi's cold winter, but everyone was friendly. They donated their used clothes, mattresses, and blankets. Sometimes the mattresses or blankets would have mites in them, and the clothes would be oversized or torn, have holes, or smell bad since they were all used and old, but Jyoti and her children could not be picky. Someone gave her an electric hotplate to cook the food since they had no way to cook food. They were also given utensils. Her parent's friends were all grandparents themselves; they understood the helplessness of a parent—Jyoti as a parent and Jyoti's parents as parents.

After a total of ten days outside the house, they got a flat in west Delhi. It was on the fourth floor, so it was also a cooler flat in West Delhi. It was on the fourth floor, so it was also colder. Walking the stairs and coming down was a task for Jyoti. It had two small rooms, a kitchen, and a bathroom. Children put the mattress on the floor to sleep, and the things given by the people—like clothes, shoes, and their second handbooks—were kept in another room. The paint on the walls was old and had black marks, similar to the walls of the DCW office. There was no geyser, so they would bathe in cold water.

This was also the neighbourhood where Jyoti's maternal home was located, so people who had been living there for twenty-five years knew her. The only change was the last glimpse of Jyoti as a newly wed bride, and now they were seeing a fifty-year-old Jyoti with four adult kids. As a substitute for ID, one of their friends helped Jyoti open a bank account without using any ID since she had a priority account there. This acted as an ID until the family applied for a copy. Their struggle with experiencing rags after being raised in riches began here.

Children started looking up for work. Karishma was going to see her master, which her mother suggested she must continue. She nevertheless started a side gig. Govind started working at a call centre, but he had just passed the twelfth grade, so he couldn't get much work. The other two sons, Krishna and Jai, started working as store managers and labourers at different shops in Chandni Chowk. These children were not street-smart; this was their first exposure to this world. The jobs that they got were also through the references of Jyoti's parents' friends. The family started making around thirty thousand per month. They started eating roti with onions or pickles since they could not afford to cook curry daily with a rent of ten thousand rupees per month. Jyoti's parents' friends or neighbours would occasionally give her their leftover curry or food so she wouldn't have to cook and could save money. The children would walk kilometres to save the rickshaw money by walking to the bus stand, which was a twenty-minute one-way walk from their house. These were the same kids who had never used public transportation before. Each of the children had one pair of jeans, so they had to be washed daily for them to wear. Jyoti used to wash them in icy cold water as soon as the kids got home so they could dry in time to wear the next day.

One month passed, and Jyoti and her children were content in this situation. The sense of freedom and peace they had found in chapatti and raw onion was much greater than what they had been getting out of those exquisite dishes at the Arora house. But Rajesh wouldn't just give up; his educated guess was that Jyoti would probably be living near her maternal home since she had a supportive ecosystem there. He hired a private detective who followed her daughter Karishma, whose college address he knew, and henceforth found the house address. Then he paid the landlord to throw out Jyoti and the children. Rajesh was trying to persuade his family to return to him, but they feared him so much that they were willing to go to any lengths to avoid him. They would do anything to escape his abuse.

The mother and children were given a week's notice to leave by the landlord; Jyoti's father then started making calls again. He found a friend of his, who was a Delhi High Court judge, had a vacant two-bedroom flat. Since he was sitting on a powerful chair, there was hope that he would not be lured by Rajesh's money. The mother and children soon shifted. That judge advised Jyoti to start a domestic violence case against Rajesh or else he would keep poking. A legal case would also ensure her and her children's security.

Following his advice, Jyoti filed a domestic violence case. A lawyer was provided to her through the District Legal Services Authority, where the government gives free legal help to those who cannot afford it. She filed her complaint on January 25, 2016. She also gave a letter to the nearest police station about the threat she and her children faced because of her husband. All this was done on the advice of her lawyer. The family continued to earn and eat on their own. Within three years, they bought clothes, a TV, an air conditioner, a washing machine, etc. on EMIs the children paid.

Fast-forwarding to the present, it's now 2022. Jyoti is fifty-five years old now, and Rajesh is sixty. Karishma is an economist today, and Govind has done his MBA and is earning well for himself. Krishna and Jai have moved to Australia, where Jyoti's sister lives; they are chefs in Sydney. Jyoti is given maintenance money per month by Rajesh; this is the money that her children now force their father to give to Jyoti since she has given her prime years to him. She travels often to Australia to see her sons. She also loves travelling solo and exploring new places. She has her own business in network marketing, which is a steady source of passive income for her. She and her children live in a three-bedroom flat in the same upscale neighbourhood as Rajesh. This is one of Rajesh's flats. It has a huge balcony where Jyoti enjoys gardening every morning while sipping her tea and enjoying the peaceful sunlight. Jyoti has internalized the fact that she might not have the support of a partner in old age. And that society would time and again question and laugh at her as to why she left her husband after twenty-five years and why not just then. But she knows her struggles, how she fought, and how she emerged as a winner. Some opined that she wasted twenty-five years, to which Jyoti replied, 'My struggle gave me the strength I possess today.'

In the domestic violence case, in the past seven years, not even one order has been passed against Rajesh. He laughs off the case, saying, 'I know the reality of the judiciary today. Can't you people see I haven't even hired a lawyer to fight on my side? I'd rather buy the judge and your lawyer. Even if the judge passes any order, I will challenge every order in the higher court. By the time the final verdict comes, I will be dead. Your mother can then prove whatever she wants.'

Rajesh's words show the reality of the administration and judiciary today. Jyoti fought the abuse with valour. She separated from her husband after twenty-five years of marriage. She motivated her children to stand on their own two feet. But the slow judicial process is prone to collusive corruption and manipulation, which stops many women from taking the step that Jyoti did. After standing up to her husband, it's now her turn to stand up to the system.

*****

Author's Message

Your past does not define you. You are not a victim; you are a survivor. You have the power to overcome and thrive beyond the pain.

6

SHIVAMMA

Ridima Vaidya

The chirping birds in our garden, the misty breeze from my bedside window flirting with my satin curtains, the smoky smell of the wood burning in our outdoor hot water boiler, the very loud arguments from our always grumpy neighbours, and the All India Radio morning broadcast with the most melodious songs summed up my childhood mornings back home. It has been almost fifteen years since I have been away from home, but I can still remember those mornings like they were yesterday.

Home for me is a small town called Sangli. In any case, I'm no longer small. Sangli is developing at the speed of light. But whether society's behaviour and thoughts can match that speed is a debatable topic.

I woke up on one such morning. I was seventeen, and it was around 7 a.m. I went to the kitchen. My mom was all cleaned up; her wet hair was made into a bun and wrapped up in a towel. Little drops of water from her hair were dripping on her shoulder, but it didn't seem to bother her as she was busy grating the ginger to the beats of the song playing on the radio. The pot of boiling tea was sitting on the burner against the kitchen window, and the sun rays passing through that steam brushed my hands as I hugged my mom good morning.

I whispered in my mom's ears, 'Mom, you know you are the best, and you make the world's best ginger tea.'

She looked at me from the corner of her eye and said, 'I am also the world's most intelligent mom, and I can sense this extra lovey-dovey buttering is for a reason. Care to share?'

I smiled and gave in with no denials. As I was getting ready to slip in the idea of our two-day overnight trip to Mahabaleshwar, we were interrupted by the sound of the opening of our main gate. Me and my mom both looked at each other and said together, "Shivamma".

Shivamma was our house help. Sunrise could perhaps be late by a minute or two, but Shivamma would be at her doorstep at 7:10 a.m. every day. We had a window in our kitchen overlooking the main gate. I saw her walking in her usual saree. It was about four inches above her ankle and always had a black blouse underneath with its sleeves running up to her elbows and fully covering her back up to her neck. She used to wear a four-layered *mangal sutra*, three white lines of *vibhuti* across her forehead, and a big red *bindi* made of *kumkum* at the centre of these three lines. Her hair would always be soaked in coconut oil and tied tight in a bun. Her feet were covered in a heavy pyjama, the rhythm of which was generally indicative of her mood.

Her voice sounded heavy that day. Apart from her usual getup, she was wearing sunglasses, which looked a little funny with her attire. I tried cracking a joke about it, but my mom's raised brow was enough of an indication that I should shut up. My mom walked up to her and held her shoulder, and Shivamma burst into tears and hugged my mom tight. My mom surprisingly didn't ask her a thing, but the way she was holding her, it felt like she knew what had happened.

Shivamma had been working for us for twelve years at that point. She must have been about twenty-two when she first came to our place. Some random aunty from our society had brought her home because Shivamma was looking for a job. She had recently moved to Sangli from her village, Nandoor, with her husband and her two daughters. Her husband, Eknath, had decided to make this move to make some extra cash as farming wasn't helping them meet their needs. Eknath had a friend who had promised him a job in the market yard. He kept his promise and appointed him as a labourer to load and unload goods, very commonly known as a *hamal* in any Maharashtrian region. Eknath started off well with his job. Additionally, Shivamma started working as a housekeeper at two different places, one of which was ours. Eknath was fond of his two girls, but he very strongly wanted a son. Being fond of your child is different from being proud of them. He believed he could feel that pride from a boy child and continued to press Shivamma for another child. Shivamma, on the other hand, stood her ground and refused to have another baby.

When I opened up to my mom, she said, 'Didi, if it were only about having another child, I would have done it, but it is not. It is all about having a boy. What if it is a third girl for us? I cannot make her suffer the hate for not being a boy.'

The depth of her thoughts, her courage to take her own decisions, and her determination to make her girls independent were astonishing. It came from someone who had grown up in an ultra-conservative environment with no academic opportunities. Perhaps real-life experiences define such people. Those who dare to question life and strive to find a reason for their existence stand out bravely like Shivamma.

Shivamma's girls were about my age. Whenever they would come to our place along with her, we would play, chat, and study. Shivamma never let them help her with housekeeping duties. She would always say, 'I do this because I don't have a choice. I will never let my girls choose this life for themselves. They will study hard and land some respectable jobs.'

Eknath was never on board with this thought of hers. His thoughts reflected the strong influence that conservative society had left on him. He believed that girls could only do so much before returning home to care for their families.

About four years after they moved to Sangli from Nandoor, Eknath realized Shivamma was never going to say yes to another child. His frustration started building up; he started drinking and became inconsistent at picking shifts at the market yard. His employer almost terminated him for being a no-show a couple of times.

Shivamma eventually became the breadwinner for the family. She had made it clear to Eknath that she was working extremely hard to provide for her family, and she would not accept a single penny for alcohol. She had to face many fights with Eknath because of this, which turned into regular domestic violence later. My mom suggested several times to turn him in, but Shivamma would always say, 'He is good at heart, Didi. Just frustrated.'

Now, when I think of that statement, it makes me believe in the saying that "Love is blind". It was so unlikely for someone as strong and sorted as Shivamma to give that man the benefit of the doubt—that he would come back to his normal self someday.

Given Eknath's behavioural patterns, Shivamma realized that she was the one who needed to look out for their girls' future. She started planning for it when they were four and five years old. While she was working as domestic help at two places, she started assisting at a local tailor shop for some practical first-hand experience. Eventually, when she mastered the art, my mother bought her a sewing machine, and she started taking tailoring orders on her own. She would finish working at the two places by 3 p.m. and then go home, cook dinner, play with the girls, and work on the tailoring jobs until midnight. She started making good savings from her tailoring business. She had no knowledge of how to earn an appreciation for these savings. My dad helped her choose the right investment programs, and she started investing the money for her two daughters to get good returns by the time they turned twenty-one. While she was building the financial base for her long-term goals, she wanted to make sure that she did not lose sight of her short-term goals. She assured me that her daughters do not lack academically. They used to attend the government school, and Shivamma would bring the girls to our house during my study sessions with Mom. She used to have frequent chats with Mom about their progress, their weaknesses, and how they could improve. Shivamma did not have a formal education, but she was unconsciously following the rules that are taught in universities to have short-term goals, long-term goals, and financial planning. She was a natural!

During these years of struggle, she was constantly fighting the battle against domestic violence with Eknath. Shivamma had become financially independent, and Eknath was losing his importance in the family, and he did not like it. Domestic violence was his way of satisfying his ego and having power over Shivamma. His family was pressuring them to move back to Nandoor. Eknath was in favour of moving back, while Shivamma was not. She knew if she moved back with the girls, the next thing that would happen was that the family would get the girls married, and they would end up having no opportunities for a successful career.

The reason I remember that morning when Shivamma was wearing the sunglasses is that the night before, Eknath's family had come to Shivamma's place, and they forced her to pack her bags and leave with them. Eknath beat her in front of the whole family, and nobody supported Shivamma. She hit the corner of a table, and her eye started bleeding internally. That is when she decided and told Eknath, 'This is enough. Stay away from me, or I am turning you and your family in. Do not dare ruin my daughters' future. I am working around the clock to give them everything you and I could not have, and I will not let you take it away in a heartbeat. You take one more step towards me, and I am calling the police.'

She was past her tolerance, and Eknath knew it was time to back off or he would end up in jail. Thereafter, Eknath moved back to Nandoor with his family, and Shivamma and the two girls decided to stay in Sangli and live life on their own terms.

As her daughters started approaching their teens, she wanted them to choose a career path and work towards it. Like mothers, like daughters. The girls had been brought up in such tough situations that they were more mature than any other kids in their age group. Both had clarity about what they wanted in life. Her older daughter, Rajshri, wanted to get into the police force to make sure there were no other Shivammas in society who must face daily domestic violence. The younger one, Indu, had grown fond of Shivamma's tailoring skills. So, she decided to pursue a career in fashion designing. Shivamma made every effort to get them in touch with the right mentors who could guide them to achieve their dreams. While this was happening, her tailoring business was booming. She had moved her business from her home to a rented shop. She quit her job as a domestic helper and went full-time into the tailoring business. Even when she quit her job at our place, she would visit Mom daily. My parents and I were like family to her, and she always remembered how my mom and dad supported her during her tough times.

Today, a few years later, Rajshri has cleared the UPSC exam and become an IPS officer, whereas Indu has launched her own label and works with top models who showcase her work. Shivamma still runs her tailoring shop and continues to preserve her identity. Eknath died from over-drinking a few years ago.

If it were not for Shivamma's determination, her family would have fallen to pieces.

*****

Author's Message

You are Powerful! Just believe in your inner strength, and you will get through it against all the odds!

7

BETRAYAL OF LOVE & TRUST

Pernel

Time flies by so quickly. We somehow fail to realize this as we get so caught up in our day-to-day cares, worries, struggles, and responsibilities that we very often fail to notice the golden years of life passing by.

So today, when I look back at my life through the lens of time, I see a shy and quiet girl, the eldest sibling in a family of five. Brought up in a loving and caring atmosphere, it was here where I imbibed the values of honesty, transparency, and strong family bonds.

My parents had an inter-caste marriage, and when you look back at the 1970s, you realize that it could not have been easy for my dad, who was a Muslim, to make the decision to convert to Christianity and give up ancestral property just to marry my mom. She, being a staunch Catholic, inculcated in us a strong faith in God, which ultimately gave me the inner strength to overcome adversities. I had seen them make sacrifices just to give us a better life. Unconsciously, I realized that true love means making sacrifices for those whom we love the utmost.

At a very young age, when I fell in love with a boy, I refused to give up on him even though I was aware that he had a few vices, and that was the reason my parents didn't approve of him. Not wanting to hurt them, I repeatedly tried to convince them, and they got me married after I had completed my graduation.

With sweet dreams of living a life of joy and togetherness, we began our life's journey, and within the first year, I sensed that my world had gone topsy-turvy. I began to realize that there was a vast difference in our family values and upbringing. A keen sense of responsibility was surprisingly missing in him. Being the youngest of his siblings and the only son, he was extremely pampered and often misled.

My in-laws found fault with everything I did, no matter how hard I tried to please them. I found myself left alone as my husband was never there; he was staying in another city for work. I was subjected to mental torture from my mother-in-law's verbal abuse, as she would drink every night and become violent and break things, and to add the cherry on top, I was pregnant with my first child. I knew that this atmosphere was not conducive to raising a child, but I couldn't do much about it then.

I cried and prayed every night, but nothing changed. The day I delivered my baby girl, my husband was away, travelling to Mumbai for an interview to work on a cruise ship. My family was always there for me. So, while my husband was away, I went to live with my parents, as my mother-in-law refused to take care of the baby while I was at work.

At first, I thought I had gained some peace of mind, but I soon discovered that my husband had added heavy drinking, smoking, casino gambling, and dating girls on the ship as young as sixteen and seventeen years old, to his list of vices. When I confronted him, he casually said that he just took these girls around to explore the places when the ship docked at a port. Otherwise visiting casinos and strip bars was just for timepass. It seemed so casual, that he wasted his hard-earned money on these luxuries, and I struggled to give him an account of every single paisa of the three thousand rupees he would send me every month to manage the household.

When he came home during his vacation, nothing changed as he visited gambling dens and wouldn't show up for days sometimes. He had no time for his daughter, either. I somehow sensed that he had gone too far to turn back, but I had to endure for the sake of my daughter. I tried to talk to him about being a little more responsible as a dad since we didn't even have a house of our own and I was still staying with my parents. But it was all in vain; his sugar-coated words would persuade me, but his actions never matched his words.

I was pregnant for the second time. This time, he was at home during the delivery of my son, but surprisingly, he was nowhere to be found at the hospital. My mom tried calling him several times, but his phone was switched off. All I knew was that he was never there when I needed him the most.

We rented a house near my school since I felt that we needed to spend some quality time alone to bond better. It had been almost four months since he had come home, and things kept getting worse. The verbal abuse, the drinking, the gambling, and, to add to things, when I came home from school one fine day, things did not look normal. My baby son was crying uncontrollably, the maid had left, my husband was behaving very peculiarly, and the maid didn't turn up for a few days. I got word from my neighbour that he had sex with the maid and was threatening her to keep her mouth shut. How low could this man stoop? I just asked myself. When I confronted him, he created a ruckus and defended himself by blaming the maid. Anyways, I got rid of the maid and started doing the household chores myself with two kids to look after with no help from him. I had to manage the household with my meagre earnings. My life had already become a nightmare!

Whenever I inquired about his return to the ship, he would always become defensive and give me vague answers. Ultimately, one day, in a fit of rage, he said that he had a fistfight with a fellow colleague, and both of them were expelled from the ship. It struck as a bolt from the blue. I got to know this after almost six months! Things went downhill from here, as he had already squandered the money that he had with him. All my gold jewellery was missing, and the plot of land that we had bought was lost due to his addiction to gambling. I got word from the landlady that he had already taken back the deposit amount. It was shocking! I had sleepless nights; where would we go? This was the question on my mind.

Amidst all this chaos, I always had a word with God and would ask him just one simple question: 'Why me? Of all the scheming and nasty people in the world, why would you choose a young, innocent girl to go through this? Never in my wildest dreams did I ever imagine that this is what life would turn out to be.' I would tell myself, 'Welcome to the Jungle,' where the strongest survives, not with physical strength but with mental strength, grit, and endurance!

I was in a small one-room kitchen with all of the necessities. My husband took up a job, and I thought that it was a good start. The first month, all seemed well; he would come home after work and have time for the family, but as a few months progressed, his behaviour started to become erratic. He started coming home very late, was often drunk and abusive, and did not give any money for monthly expenses. One night, his boss tapped on my door at around midnight. I was surprised because I thought it was my husband. He informed me that after work hours, my husband had brought back one of his colleagues to the office, and they were caught in a compromising position by some of the local boys who found their behaviour suspicious. It was not surprising anymore! In fact, it was a pattern, and I had missed the red flags.

In that part of the night, I took both my kids and went to my parents' house. He eventually came there at around 2 a.m., and when I confronted him, once again he denied that he ever had an affair. He lied again and again that the boys had some personal grudge and animosity. That was the very moment I realized it cannot be love when a man has the audacity to look into your eyes and lie to you. I stayed for a while with my parents, and I cried and prayed every day for a miracle to happen and for him to have a change of heart. I was in a dilemma. 'What now? Should I leave him? What will my children go through without a father? What will society say? and finally, what is it that I want to do?'

So, I finally decided that I needed to stand on my own two feet and get a stable job if I wanted to give my children a better life. I gave the CET exam and got admission for a B.Ed. degree in Mumbai, which was eventually financed by my dad. My children were left with my parents, and both of us came to Mumbai to start afresh. I stayed with my brother, and I thought it would be easier for him to get a job here. My brother would give us pocket money for my travel expenses and for him to look for a job for an entire year; surprisingly, he did not get a job for an entire year. After completing my B.Ed., I rented a flat, got a job as a teacher in an affluent school, managed to get admission for my kids in the same school, and my husband surprisingly got a job in a call centre. I thought I could forget the past and begin a new life just for my kids. For almost a year, everything was not too bad, but then a gambling den was discovered, and my husband managed to make a few friends.

Within the next six months, the vices raised their ugly heads again and ruined everything. One day, when I came home from work, my daughter was crying. Her father manipulated her and forcefully took the gold earrings from her ears. Slowly, it was my earrings and then my wedding ring, followed by physical abuse for not adhering. He lost his job again and needed money for drinking and gambling. I found myself going back to square one. My children were not happy, their studies were affected, and I was having sleepless nights, sometimes waiting for him to come home. He left and went after a few days, claiming that his mother was ill and needed someone to care for her, but I later learned that he was having an affair with someone back in my hometown, with the support of his family.

Somewhere in the back of my mind, I realized that I and my kids were happier without him, as I was the one doing everything for them, and most of all, there was peace at home. He came back after a few months, and for some lame excuse, he physically assaulted me. That was the last straw. I went straight to the police station and lodged a complaint for domestic violence. He was asked to leave Mumbai and go back to my hometown, as I was paying all the bills and the rent.

It was only due to the support of my family that I was able to survive the crisis. Today, it will be almost thirteen years since I separated, but I have never regretted my decision for even a single day in my life. The moment I focused my attention on my kids, I knew that I wanted to give them the childhood that my parents gave me. It wasn't easy; I was physically exhausted from being on my feet from 4.30 a.m. to midnight at times. But it gave me joy, and most importantly, I had found my peace of mind after many years. I didn't care what the world said about me or what false rumours were spread about me by my in-laws. All I knew was that whatever I was doing was best for my kids, and that was my priority. I always believed that "Time will tell". Like the weeds are separated from the harvest! Amidst all this, I got to know that my daughter has a learning disability; I got the required tests and counselling sessions done, and I myself did a diploma course to identify learning disabilities and slow learners. Today, I help the children in my school. My daughter has graduated in mass media and is pursuing advanced graphic designing; my son is a computer engineer; and I am a proud MOM!

I also found the answer to the question, "Why me"? So as a teacher, I would always assign the most difficult task to the student I could trust the most because I know that she is capable of executing it to the best of her ability. God does the same! He knows each one of us.

*****

Author's Message

A message for all those women who are going through similar situations in life and are worried about society, shame, prestige, or anything else, just remember one thing: You have only one life; give it your best shot. Never give up or give in to being humiliated or belittled in life. Always remember that trust and respect are the foundation of every relationship!

8

A LETTER TO MY DAD

authorneelima

Nowadays, everyone is growing, society is growing, and the literacy rate is increasing everywhere in the world. People are focusing on education and technology. Several ideas have been developed and implemented by mankind. But still, in some places, people are living a restricted life, and they are not even willing to grow. They are stuck in their stereotypical mindset. These stigmatized individuals experience anxiety, which depletes their cognitive resources.

There is one type of stereotype that is associated with giving unnecessary attention to men and degrading women in society. They think that because he is a man, he has all the rights. Because he is a man, he is free to speak anything and do anything. They don't even think about whether men are right or wrong; they just blindly follow them without even giving it a second thought.

On the other hand, there is another stereotype due to which society feels that because she is a woman, she cannot do certain things: she cannot walk alone; she cannot run a house; she should not have her own individual opinions. With this mindset in place, women continue to face problems, and this social mentality is dragging them down and preventing them from progressing in their lives. Sometimes, it is very hard for a woman to pursue what she wants to do in her life.

Along with that, there is another version of this society where people are dual-faced and hypocritical. These kinds of people are different in different places. When they are in public, they say that they are so open-minded; they give all the freedom to women and don't differentiate between a man and a woman. But, when they are inside their houses and when it comes to supporting their daughters, wives, and sisters, they also start showing their second version. So, these people are also the same, but they just try to hide their real selves from this society; in the end, they support men, particularly men with tags.

They don't even want to use their heads when they see a man coming with a tag. They think a man with a tag is always right. A man with a tag always does the right thing, always makes the right decisions, and is always nice to everyone.

Sometimes, life is so complicated. We face numerous challenges and encounter a variety of circumstances. But for Vamika, life is full of surprises and challenges. She feels everyone is capable enough to deal with life's ups and downs.

Whenever she is confused and wants to discuss something or wants to make any big decision in her life, she just talks with her dad because he is her hero. Every time she feels low, she just seeks out her dad's motivational words, although her dad is a politician and a very busy person and doesn't get enough time as he is always surrounded by lots of people.

Her dad is an optimistic and opinionated person. Whatever the topic, her dad always has something to suggest or say, as he has also gone through ups and downs in his life. So, he has a lot of experience with everything. He always says, 'Just do your work; God will take care of the rest.'

Vamika always talks with her dad and discusses everything with her parents, though they never have the same opinions. If one talks about the south, the other talks about the north. If there is a glass filled half with water, then for Vamika, it is half full, and for her dad, it is half empty. Though they both have the same mindset, they have different opinions about it.

Her father has found so many good guys for her over the last three years, but she has never liked whoever her father has chosen for her. When she realized this, she also started finding someone for herself, as she thinks her life partner should be a guy who makes her life comfortable and peaceful.

Vamika and her father had numerous arguments and discussions following each rejection. Once they had a big argument, and they both stopped talking to each other for almost a year.

Vamika used to miss her dad. One day, she couldn't stop herself. So, she wrote a letter and poured all her emotions into it, then sent it to her dad.

LETTER

My dear Papa,

In our society, everyone thinks a man with a tag is probably the right choice for any woman. Previously, I used to feel the same. So, I always wanted to marry a man with a good tag, like someone from India's top institute, whether it is an IIM or an IIT guy. Even to this day and age, old people believe that if a man comes up with a tag, he is a righteous person in every way. People don't even care whether that person is mindful or whether he is able to handle critical situations in his life or not. Whether he is respectful to women or not, whether he has been raised like a good man or not

Even though I found a few men with tags, those men rejected me. I don't know why they rejected me, whether because of my face or because of my behaviour. I had been trying to ask them what the reason for this rejection is, where I am lacking, and what I should improve. I begged you to give me another chance so I could work on my flaws and become a better person. I can change myself.

Even after so many requests, no one stayed with me. On top of that, they humiliated, disrespected, and misbehaved with me, and a few of them laughed at me. I felt like I was nothing to them; I couldn't even justify myself, my hard work, or my achievements.

One man with an IIM tag came and showered love and affection on me. I fell in love the moment I saw all of this. I thought he was as good as his tag. Once, he captured my video in an inappropriate situation. At that time, I trusted him and assumed that, along with his tag, he was a good human being. But after a month of showing that video, he started blackmailing me. He literally tried to spoil my career and life as well.

At that point in my life, for the first time, I realized it's not a sure thing that a man with a good tag will also be a good person.

After this failure, I was depressed for many months. I was struggling and thinking, 'What am I missing? I have worked hard in my life and achieved a lot. Even with all these things, I don't deserve a good life partner. I was questioning God; I was blaming myself for everything.'

Later, I was thinking about my status and analysing my situation in the family. Then, I came to the conclusion that you and other family members also have numerous problems with me. No one wants to chill with me. No one wants to stay with me. Even on big festivals and occasions, no one even called me home in the last three years.

I have been thinking:

What is the meaning of my life?

What is the meaning of "working hard"?

What is the meaning of these achievements?

At that time, my achievements looked like nothing to me. I used to feel everything was worthless, including my existence. No one cared whether I was alive or dead.

I travelled to different places; I went to parties; I went to NGOs. I met with people of different ages, with aunties and kids, and I learned about different cultures and languages. I had tried so many things to get out of this. I lived with the hope that one day someone would be happy with me and that someone would appreciate my deeds.

Instead of giving up, every day I tried so many new things to be alive and to keep myself motivated because I don't like quitters. One day, I got to know that my friends had bought a pet parrot, an Australian breed, and they named it Alita. So, I decided to go out and play for a while with their bird. I thought that after seeing and playing with it, if I liked it, I would also get something like that for diverting myself.

I met another man and his sister, along with their pet Alita. His name was AJ. That man came and talked with me. They all appeared to be such nice, good people. So, I invited them for tea at my place. We gradually began to meet each other for tea and became good friends.

One day, I went to meet my new friends and their parrot, Alita. At that time, I was overwhelmed, so I shared my story with them. After telling my story, I started crying like hell. I cried a lot, and I cried continuously for six hours. After some time, I slept. They all left me sleeping in a room, and they got occupied with their stuff; some of them were watching TV in the hall.

After getting depressed for more than six months, I decided to get rid of that feeling. Due to my bereavement and embarrassment, when I woke up, I tried to kill myself. But suddenly AJ came and stopped me and screamed at me:

'Stupid lady, I will always be with you, I promise; I will never leave you like others.'

After handling that situation maturely, we all became good friends and started going for tea together. A few months later, I shifted with them to their apartment. In a few days, that guy and his sister started making me feel at home, and their family also started talking to me.

We once took a road trip to AJ's hometown. There we met his family members. His family treated me with love and respect. They gave me a lot of attention and respect, which I never got in my family. His family was so good. In their home, they kept me like a celebrity for three days. Those three days are still the best days of my life.

Once I came back, I was so happy, so motivated, and full of positive energy. One day I got an idea. I discussed it with my friends and seniors, and everyone praised it.

AJ supported me in implementing it at the ground level, and later he helped me in selling it, as he is the best person for marketing and selling something.

In between all of my career decisions, AJ proposed to me, but in order to settle my company, I needed to relocate to a new city. AJ, on the other hand, was there for me every step of the way. That's how I started my own company, and today everyone knows about my brand and my name.

When I was moving to a new place, AJ again proposed to me, and then I said, 'Try to settle in the same town, and then I will marry you.'

Then I came to the new place, got busy with my company work, and settled my things. I and AJ were still in touch, and he used to say he was working on things, but after a few months, he would also come to my place.

In this phase, I was very frustrated, as I was in a new place and giving trials on new things related to my work in my own company. In all the worst situations and mood swings, AJ was always there to support me, and he supported me the way he promised and kept his words, which he uttered to me one year ago.

After a year and lots of talks, fights, discussions, and arguments, he finally settled in at my place. Previously, I assumed that he would never come to my place, and once I reached here, I would also forget him. But nothing like this happened. He was always there to support me, and he always helped me whenever I needed it. He took care of this relationship, and he proved himself a reliable person for the relationship.

He took a remote job and stayed with me at my place so that he could support me. For me, he left his family, his settled life, and his career and came here with me. Who else would do all this? Who has dared to leave everything for a woman? How many guys in India compromise for their partners?

In the end, I want to conclude that he is a good guy; I feel comfortable with him; he fits this relationship. He never left me alone; he values words, people, and relations. He knows how to handle everything in life.

We always need a person who can stand by our side in any situation in life. So, in my words, I want to marry him. Please accept him. Let's start with other verifications and preparations for my marriage.

I hope this time you will support me and praise me for something I have done or someone I have chosen because for me you are always my priority, and I always remember you whenever I need support or make big decisions.

When I was failing in my life at all times, I used to say that if nothing worked, I would leave everything and go to my hometown. My father would undoubtedly assist me in some way. I trust him and his capabilities.

So, as AJ also said, just as you trust your dad, similarly, I trust you. I believe that even if nothing worked and I failed, you would always be there for me and support me.

Papa, he trusted me in his life as much as I trusted you in mine. So, I don't know what else I need in my life other than this. At least now I am not useless to someone.

Thanks,

Your daughter

Vamika

*****

That's how Vamika confronts her dad. She wants to marry a person who has supported her in bad times because real friends and companions are the ones who support you in your bad times. Otherwise, this world is full of fake and foolish men with tags.

It's okay if you are sad today; tomorrow, definitely, you will laugh. So, just don't worry, be relaxed, and live each phase of your life fully. What matters most is what you learn and how you apply your knowledge later in life.

*****

Author's Message

At last, I reflect that a man who treats others respectfully is a real man, not a man with tags.

9

TO BE OR NOT TO BE

Charvi Jain

'Hello there!'

Allow me to introduce myself slowly. For the time being, dear reader, all you need to know is that I am a regular person. My distinction is biological.

I am an extremely pleasant person with an intellect in which I take great pride. I had a generous and prosperous career in real estate, which was also where I met my adored yin to the yang, my wife Morana. We have been blessed with two healthy and beautiful twins, my darling boy Xander and my princess Amara.

But I must confess to you, my reader, that I, Tristan Heyward Venmore, have placed my job, position, and authority in the hands of my wife and have become a full-fledged househusband! The best thing is... I wouldn't change it for the world.

Two and a half years later....

As I try to feed my dear Amara her breakfast, I sit on the edge of my stool, my tongue sticking out, my eyes squinting, and my hair a jumble of peas, pineapple, and yoghurt. My wife, Morana, all clad in one of her power suits, strides into the dining area and doubles over laughing. Keeping the yoghurt out of Amara's reach, I stand up and head to the kitchen aisle, where Morana's breakfast, her lunch, and her secret dinner are packed along with the vitamin medicines. Like clockwork, I go outside to the nursery to wake up my sleepy-headed son, thinking to myself how his kids are the exact opposite of one another, even after being born out of the same womb and entering the world at the same time.

I run back to see my wife juggling her laptop bag, lunch boxes, and phone while tickling our kid and promising to return shortly. She then turns her attention to me, and I feel an overpowering sense of pride. As I send her off, I tell her about the dinner tonight with our families and their family friends, and all I get is a brief nod as she takes off.

I get why you're confused. You know, around two and a half years ago, I suffered significant losses in my real estate business, which rocked the core of the empire that I had worked so hard to build. It took a severe emotional and physical toll on me, bringing me to the verge of suicide.

Despite this, I met my wife, Morana, and a patron who was seeking an Upper East Side apartment in New York. One meeting grew into two, and the second resulted in her moving into my house six months later, and everything has been concluded now. Morana had not only conquered my heart, but she had also utilized her interpersonal and intellectual talents to assist me in discovering flaws in the firm. We had repaired error after error, talked to client after client, and restored the heritage of "Heyward Laurentis Firms" to its former glory one by one.

"The night of the incident", as I've come to call it, and the weeks that followed were when I realized Morana's true potential. After long discussions and arguments, possibly even fights, we agreed on her taking the lead of the company instead of me. I stayed comfortably domesticated and took care of the family. 'Fair exchange,' as I like to say.

But, even if we have the ability to think, analyze, and solve problems, the wavelengths of society and one's belief system end up colliding in a pit of darkness and malice. Let me explain how.

That evening….

'Hi Tristan, I'll be a little late for the family meet-and-greet. Certain challenges are addressed in the policies of a major firm. If the press gets wind of this, it will be a nightmare.' Morana was on the other end of the phone an hour before their family gathering. Tristan, with a smile on his face, urged her to discover the solution and contributed his own experience, even though he was hoping she would be present. At least she hadn't absolutely answered no. Wasn't that a relief?

He dressed both of the kids, loaded them into the car, surrounded them with light snacks, and hummed all the way to their parents' house, pocketing the cell. To imply that his parents were humble was as implausible as people running on water. Oh, no! Heywards had an uncanny ability to imprint their name, reputation, and grandeur on the hearts and minds of everyone they knew. The Laurentis, on the other hand, were not wholly innocent but were willing to back down once they had solid evidence of absolute accomplishment.

'Tristan, we were just talking about you! Please come in!' Ava Heyward welcomed her son while holding a champagne bottle in her free hand. Tristan smiled and kissed her on the cheek, admired her attire, and strolled into the living room, where his in-laws and other uncles and aunts were seated. Jacob Heyward stood in the corner of the room, his gaze icy and fixed on his son. Yes, he disliked the fact that his only son had decided to be a stay-at-home father and househusband, entrusting his whole wealth to a capable but nevertheless female partner. According to him, it was syrupy, cringy, and completely undeserved.

Tristan thought to himself about this generational stereotype and scoffed at it. His in-laws both smiled warmly at him and pointedly stared behind him, waiting for their daughter. 'Morana called; she said she'll be joining us later and that we don't have to stay up and eat dinner,' he said to the children as they rustled around among their grandparents.

Jacob sneered and sipped his drink while his mother smiled and added, 'Do you know how long it'll take? Make a phone call and inquire. If she may leave now, there are visitors who are eager to meet her.'

Tristan just rolled his eyes and dialled her number, which beeped when it got to voicemail. He didn't abandon her, and he left her to finish her work without stress.

An hour slipped into two, and before you knew it, it was 11 p.m. Morana was nowhere to be found. Jacob summoned Tristan to his office, where he noticed his mother and in-laws sitting on either side. 'You see, son, I've always been proud of the way you established your business. You handled the company quite effectively. And, while I appreciate your need to rest and recover from that dreadful accident, don't you think it's about time you get back out there?' His father appeared serious.

'I agree with your father, honey; it's time to let Morana experience motherhood, visit parties, and run the family, isn't it?' His mother admonished him from behind. 'I heard my friends talking today, and they stated we should let Morana stay at home since the twins may have separation anxiety and psychiatric difficulties later in life because they were deprived of their mother in their early stages.'

His father-in-law spoke out from the other side of the room. 'I believe and trust in my daughter; she is capable of running the business, but she needs balance. Tristan, it makes little difference whether one's life and marriage become business arrangements. Try speaking to her.'

And that's how he got home. He chuckled as he unlocked his

doorway and flipped on the lights. Morana was sitting right there on their lavish couch. She was stretched out in all the glory of the steel grey suit she had worn this morning, her spectacles sideways on her face, sleeping carelessly. Nevertheless, the dinner phrase lingered in his mind like a dark cloud. He put his already sleeping children into their beds and carried Morana into hers.

Tristan lay awake in his bed that night, contemplating and rethinking everything in vivid detail, from the moment of the accident until the present. He reflected on how many times she had missed dinner, planned dates, long-forgotten excursions, and the questions his children had asked him when she had to skip their PTA meetings and parental contests. At the same time, he pondered how she had returned home late many times, dead weary and with sunken eyes, and still remained up reading stories to their children, or how she had fallen asleep in the middle of a discussion after a long day at work.

All of this made him realize how much they had both surrendered. Even though his family had said some terrible things to him, he couldn't dispute that he was happier and healthier than he had ever been.

He closed his eyes and thought about how Morana handled things on a daily basis to properly analyze the issue. This came naturally to him because he had previously dabbled in the corporate world and was now well-informed in the domestic sphere as well. Taking a deep breath, he imagined her dealing with some difficult clients, managing a position of power and doing it so skilfully, coming home, helping around the house, spending time with the kids, catching up on minor tasks that turned into all-nighters, and yet waking up every day with a beautiful smile on her face, ready to face the world.

He was aware of how cruel the world is. He was well aware that the mothers at his children's school both envied and admired their relationship and her abilities. He was aware that her parents had complete faith in her abilities and had expressed their concerns in such a generational manner. He knew his parents loved him, although he also needed to project an aristocratic image in order to keep the so-called "society" pleased.

But in the end, when he was on the verge of death due to everything in his life collapsing around him, they hadn't come to save him—not his mother, whom he adored beyond measure, nor his father, who had shown nothing but worry and disappointment in him, not his friends or the society in whose eyes an image meant everything—it was her, his wife, his lovely Morana.

There are some points in our lives that are the lowest of the lows; some call them negatives, some compare them to failures, but I call them moments of darkness. Yet, as the myth goes, 'Follow the light at the end of the tunnel,' he had seen his wife and her skill set and her balance in a much brighter light than ever before.

Gratitude is a funny thing. You never know how much you are thankful for until you lay yourself bare, without any judgements or interventions, and just allow yourself to feel; to be in the moment. To allow those feelings to ripple through our bodies like a heavy stone of reality being thrown into a river of toughness within one.

That night, he slept soundly, knowing that his worth, his decision to be a househusband, and the weight of his decision to perform the most basic of tasks like picking up toys scattered around the house, folding laundry, going to the grocery store, and effortlessly picking up ripe vegetables and fruits didn't instil any feelings of regret or embarrassment. Rather, he felt delighted at the prospect of organically settling and adjusting to such a role.

'In the end, dear reader, I urge you to be the man of the house by honestly handling the ropes of domestic tasks just as we men take satisfaction in handling the office business. There is no greater thrill than obtaining fresh vegetables at a low cost from a large vendor than closing a million-dollar transaction within the confines of your workplace.'

Signing off,
Tristian

He folded the letter he'd written a few months after taking on this role when his emotions and fears had risen in a similar way to this night. He had preserved this tiny letter to remind himself of all that had happened to him and everything that he is today.

Morana shifted sleepily next to him. He shushed her and laughed at what he heard.

'Can we please have pancakes tomorrow? I will sign whatever contract you require. Five thousand bucks...'

So, he slept comfortably that night, putting his health and family ahead of pride and arrogance.

*****

Author's Message

We often talk about human development, and we take pride in the concept of evolution. While living in a society, we like to build various rules and regulations that define how some things have to be followed and passed on. But it is the nature of societies and cultures to be dynamic. This means that change is constantly taking place. In today's world, several opportunities have given both men and women an advantage, allowing them to venture into each other's predefined roles that were based on biology, which forced them to follow the ways of society. I hope that this is one of those stories that can make every reader glad that we are slowly evolving into a beautiful, opportunistic society where men and women are equal.

10

WANDERING ABOUT A SCANDALIZED ROAD

Charvi Jain

A faint sound of footsteps filled the awfully quiet room. This quietness may appear welcoming to some, but not to me. For me, silence meant waiting—long hours of waiting with no one around, no light, no hope, no breath of fresh air. Just me and the distant thunk, thunk, thunk, of footsteps.

I awoke with a start, gasping for air and clutching my heaving chest. Shaking off the vibrations and the awful stillness creeping up my spine, I forced myself to stand. The time on the clock above said 4:44 a.m. In the last few years, putting on my running shoes while half asleep has become second nature to me.

Nights like these forced me to run without any gear for miles and miles until my chest hurt from the insufficient oxygen. The pain you see was appreciated.

On a normal day, to any normal person, it would seem like any other normal professor was going about his normal day teaching his normal class about whatever normal subject had to be taught.

But what made me different were the voices. The sounds of my past echoed deep within my very soul. After all, as they say, 'You can take the boy out of the country, but never the country out of the boy.'

Complicated huh? That was exactly what I called my life.

As I went about my supposedly normal day, taking up coffee and heading up the stairs of Willobergs University, my paradise and my nightmare, a hauntingly beautiful, spacious land that resembled any catalogue out of the woodsy Roman Institute of Education, I headed to the first class of the day.

This was life, day in and day out. The loop of the life that I had created for myself Was I the same?

No.

Would I ever be one?

Probably.

If you had asked what made me this way and the reason behind my talking in such a manner, you would have had to take a dive into my cherished past. A past in which I was the sole perpetrator of everything.

People say that abuse is something that others do to you. But what they often forget is that abuse can often be done by you too. It's a little of both for me. The lunch bell rang for a good thirty seconds, and all students dispersed from their respective classes. I visited the university's lovely gardens. Willowbergs's. Isn't that a cool name? I sat down on the usual stone bench below the usual oak tree.

I know you don't understand how this was usual, but you would.

Munching on my sandwich, I went back to my thoughts. I called this a turtle spiral—the thought vortex. The turtle spiral is something ancient and slow to pass, but once inside, time loses all meaning. John Green is wonderful in these terms. I drowned. Twenty years ago…

I opened my eyes and saw the cracked ceilings in my dormitory. My dorm was at the same university where I was a prestigious professor at the time. You must be wondering why I am talking like this. How did I become aware? How am I able to differentiate between the reality of my mind and the reality that my mind wants me to believe? My therapist called this an "out of body experience", where the memories just swarmed me, and I found myself to be the third person in my own life.

'DANINN!' exclaimed Dayana. I heard my younger sister rush around giggling as we passed through the crowd on a late Saturday evening. 'Aaahh, Daya, what is it? We are supposed to look cool, baby sister; you know I love you, but don't shoo away all the ladies, woman.' I nagged and teased my younger sister, Dayana, in equal measure. The thing about Daya was that, when you were with her, you just could not seem to hate her. No matter how she was, all of her emotions made me feel extremely protective yet understanding of her. You could say that she was the social butterfly, the life of the party. Daya, my sweet little one!

I inhaled the surroundings of my cafeteria. A faint wisp of delectable goodness floated around us. Daya couldn't be more excited to get digging into her food. I found myself face to face with Killian Collins, the most beautiful girl on the planet, as she rushed past me, a blur of happy and jumpy intertwined. She was in our grade and lived down the hall from the dorm Daya and I shared. I had seen Daya speak to her on multiple occasions, but they did not seem close, and I hadn't considered myself a victim of the wonders of infatuation.

'She sure knows how to keep herself happy, huh,' said Killian beside me. I froze. Gathering myself together when all I could hear was 'Oh my gosh, it's Killian' screaming from within, I turned to her and said, 'Trust me, a woman like her can do no wrong to herself.' I had no doubt in my mind that she would trade me one of those dumplings right there for free!

Killian released the most beautiful laugh I could have ever heard. 'My name is Killian, and I know you know who I am. It's a boy's name, but my mother loved her books, and I was named after her all-time favourite character before I was born in the hopes that I'd be a boy, but, oh well!'

Daya, at that moment, came to me with two plates in her hands, beaming as if the sun himself had rubbed off on her face. I put my hands forward to take the other one, thinking it was for me, but 'GET YOUR OWN, YOU LAZY BUM, this goodness is all minneeeeeee,' she said, and plopped on her bench, munching her food.

Killian and I, falling into the most effective banter that was impossible between two strangers to have at the first cover station, went about to get our plates, and well, soon enough, Killian and I were the best of friends.

We did the most adventurous, absurd, yet daring things together. There was no limit to what our silly little bubble could achieve. This one time, after watching a movie about mermaids and a dozen videos on YouTube of people spotting them on the beaches, we decided to use the university lake as our own Atlantis, complete with mermaid costumes and whatnot.

It doesn't matter that, looking at the three of us, a lot of people had a lot to say. Many people envied our friendship, and many were concerned that I, as a boy, wasn't behaving normally by hanging out with girls. Many guys came up to me to tease me about being a wiener and prude, but they also called me a disgusting person for engaging in such girlish habits as dressing up, doing what we wanted, and even forcing Killian to hang out with us.

Killian was the most affected by these people because Daya and I were siblings, and he accused her of interfering with the relationship by using Daya to be closer to me, a senior, and restricting me from worldly pleasures despite the fact that she wasn't in a relationship with me. Eventually, she pulled back, and it was Daya and me all over again.

Killian bursts into our room one evening in the final semester of graduate school, tears in her eyes. Screaming and shouting about how the visual club she had joined instigated a lot of uncensored activities and that it was like a cult that had no way out. She wailed over and over again about how they had roped her in and slowly introduced her to the "buyers and customers". There was no regard for their personal wishes as they had enough blackmail to ruin people's lives.

Daya calmed her down, and I looked for legal ways to deal with these issues. We involved her parents and consulted the educational institutions' guidelines and whatnot. In the midst of all of this, I was also dragged in. People gradually dragged her name into it, making claims about how she had drawn Killian in because of her vivacious personality and so on. My beautiful sister, who was so full of life... I could see the light leave her eyes. But she never stopped. Time and time again, Daya and I did everything we could to help Killian, even though it meant putting her neck on the line, but Daya never backed down on Killian.

Killian made it. But somewhere along the way, the whispers became so loud… that Daya lost herself in them. The voices, like the river Styx in Greek mythology, were the voices of the damned, the rotten, and the lingering tormentors who sucked her beautiful soul into the abyss. And she chose to put an end to it.

I remember that night really well...

Killian and I were sitting on the couch with a movie on, one of the quiet days after Killian got her freedom. Daya was supposed to be in the kitchen, popping the corn, but then a loud clatter followed by a sickening thump and a stream of red marked the tiles.

We rushed in to check what had happened, and what we saw made Killian scream in terror. On the fresh marble floor was Daya, her eyes open, staring at the dorm's ceiling, with a small smile gracing her face as she passed on.

The only thought that crossed my mind at that moment was this: 'I had not been there for her.'

Had I chosen to let go of Killian and forced Daya to cut the self-righteous loop, maybe I would not be seeing my larger-than-life sister crippled on the floor this way.

Grief like no other slammed into me. I fell on my knees, and the only sound in the room was the thump thunk thunk of the frantic footsteps caused by Killian's feet as she rushed around to Daya, screaming at me to call the ambulance and get her out. But all I could focus on was the sound that the footsteps made—a haunting melody of the day—and my life flipped. I could not hear Killian shout at me. I could not bear to see her face anymore. She'd gotten away with her haunting, but she'd left my sister's memory as a ghost.

My parents, you ask?

Daya was the wonder baby of the family. Losing her left a crack so deep in my parents' hearts that their only source of breathing was through taking it all out on me.

'You were supposed to protect her. It didn't matter that she cared about others; you had to know what was good for her.'

'We knew it was a mistake to believe you could complete such a task. Choosing family has never been one of your traits, and I bet you're glad about that.'

'Oh, look at this. Here comes the man who sold off his sister to death just so he could protect the girl that he liked.'

'You're lucky, you're a man; if you had known an ounce of what my dear Daya had gone through... you would have shown her an ounce of love and affection.'

My mother used her words, but my father used anything and everything that came within the reach of his hands or legs if I showed my face to him. Glasses, sticks, logs, even a burning poker—nothing seemed to simmer his rage towards me.

And I deserved it. I had lost my sister at the hands of the one person I wished I had never met.

I began to self-harm soon after. The voices, the memories, the yelling and shouting of my family—the same whispers that haunted my sister—and more joined the most treacherous symphony. This made me stand by the fact that I do not deserve to be forgiven and that I deserved to live a long, long life drenching myself in this weight. Death would come to me one day, but one thing was for sure: I would never go looking for it because kindness was something I did not deserve.

The buzzing of the bees brought me back to the present. I blinked quickly, wondering how deep the spiral had drawn me in again.

Twenty years...

For twenty long years, every day I visited my sister's grave to tell her the little things about my day and how sorry I was about a lot of things.

On many occasions, I talked about how I wished it was me in there instead of her. How could Mom and Dad not come down to visit or even call to see if their son was alive or not?

But Dannin wanted to get better. That's why he sought out Mr Drakesby, the best therapist he could ever ask for. It was Mr Drakesby who told him that it was alright to feel the guilt. It was alright to not be able to forgive oneself for the time being because things were too hard. That it was totally normal to feel like a victim too because of the treacherous abuse inflicted by society, the beatings that his father intentionally caused out of misdirected anger and sadness, and the abuse that he had been putting himself through all these years, blaming himself so drastically.

It is funny how small things that are shared as jokes and little taunts and are thought of as learning lessons can turn into the most jagged and broken things. They ruin lives in the blink of an eye. People whisper about a lot of things. In many ways, many topics have lost their essence of importance, especially in the case of men. 'You can't show emotions; you're a man. Show too much emotion—oh, you're a girl? Or, oh, your ego has no bounds. Be open-minded. The man doesn't value traditions and is closed and cautious. You're the most heartless soul on this planet.'

Men see, men hear, and men feel, and they feel a lot. Men have breakdowns, breakups, and issues with their identity, their appearance, and their emotions overflow, and men, too, experience various forms of abuse, seen and unseen, heard and unheard, acknowledged and unacknowledged.

But the bottom line is that… we look within ourselves to determine how we want to affect others and ourselves because IT MATTERS. YOU MATTER. YOUR STORIES ARE IMPORTANT.

*****

Author's Message

Throughout history, men have been perceived as strong, courageous, brave-hearted souls who put logical reasoning before expressing emotions. However, being closed off about how you're feeling is not the same as showing vulnerability. People in today's society are urging men to come forward, express themselves, help them cope, and tell them it's alright to talk about their abuse because, just like women, just like breathing, just like eating, drinking, and walking, men have emotions too. Men feel it too. And men get hurt too. Male abuse is such a hush-hush topic that it has turned into a stigma stemming from a rigid mental framework, and I have taken a small step in breaking this down by writing this story.

11

MODERN MIRROR

Darshana Sontakke

In the hue of existence, we have forgotten the in-betweens that life offers, where so many shades other than just black and white exist. No messed-up personas, no masquerade hidden behind a smart phone's screen—a place surrounded with oceans of love, little sorrow, and plenty of light—enough to make those eyes full of good glittery shine.

How we look defines us in today's world. A world full of so many *social mirrors*, mirrors those appear very attractive and alluring from a distance but are empty like a glass jar from the inside. These mirrors, which we cannot touch with our bare hands, yet they have caught us inside their dreamy land full of illusions, we can't escape...

Welcome to twenty-first century the "Generation Z", where everyone is the puppet of internet community. Meeting so many people from different cultures with just a touch of the phone, connecting people, they say, but disconnecting from their real selves, nobody tells!

Getting in touch with different cultures means meeting different people. When I say different, it actually means different because they are born and brought up differently. Watching so many humans and their lives creates competition that is generated naturally. Brown girls are jealous of white girls, white girls want figures like brown girls, a healthy guy wants to have biceps like that dude, a kid cannot wait to flaunt his style, and one day the envy becomes a priority to prove to the world we are no less than those perfect humans famous all over the reels, leading to "cyberbullying and body shaming". If you cannot see anything beautiful, get yourself a better "mirror"!

This story is finding each one of us who lost themselves in one perfect "Selfie", one trending "Reel", some not-so-perfect "Shots", and inappropriate "Captions". Don't you want to meet your true self again?

Bearish,

Fatty,

Overweight,

Dark,

Disastrous,

Fluff ball,

Chubby.

All of the cuss words were thrown at her in a dime a dozen. She was dig into dirt as "bold as brass" in a blink of an eye, unwillingly. What a messy trail of memories to revisit, isn't it?

Brown skin tone, shining like copper gold, eyes nut-shaped, curvy frame—a beautiful young lady who had forgotten her traits, a seventeen-year-old girl.

She is sitting lost in her room. 'Siya!' Her mother yelled. 'Come, dinner is ready, Kanna. Don't you want to eat food tonight?' But her mother's voice was not remarkable enough to drag Siya to shore from the ocean of thoughts she was sinking deep into. Ignoring her mother's caring call, Siya continued to stare at the wall of her room. Suddenly, someone knocked on the door softly. 'Are you asleep, Siya?' (Knock-Knock) It was Siya's mother right at the door; she pushed the door and noticed it was already unlatched. 'What are you doing?' she asked.

Siya looked right into her mother's eyes, suppressing all grief, and said, 'I am not hungry, Amma.'

Amma: 'What? You haven't eaten anything since daylight, Kanna. Are you okay? Well, I know how to make you jump off the bed! Guess what I have prepared tonight? What you relish the most!' Siya's mother tried to give hints in an exciting voice: 'Your favourite meal—sponge dosa and sambar.'

Siya could smell the aromatic fragrance of hot, piping sambar spreading all over the house. 'I don't like it anymore!' Siya replied in a shaking voice. 'What happened, beta?' Siya's mother asked! 'I'm worn out; I want to take a nap; please leave me alone Ma!' 'But Siya…!' 'Mom, please!' Siya interrupted, 'I insist.'

'Okay, goodnight, Kanna.' Siya's mother kissed her forehead and left the room as she closed the door patiently.

Siya took some steps towards her balcony and felt a strong flow of air touch her cheeks, so strong that it felt like a hard slap on her face. She tried to fall asleep there, sitting on the comfy chair, bending her body almost like a toddler, to escape that gloomy outlook.

'What a fatty!'

'How can you wear such clothes?'

'Look at her, what a shame!'

'That dress doesn't fit you, girl!'

'You look funny!'

But the words put on her picture, which poked and wrenched Siya's heart and shattered her miserably, were,

'Go look yourself in the mirror; you have no right to wear this; you are not worth it!'

Commented a twenty-one-year-old guy "Shaan", wealthy, famous, and very good-looking. Who had all the luxuries in the world at his feet.

'Stop it! Will you?' Siya shouted as she opened her eyes in anger; no one was there to hear her painful scream, but only immense darkness. It was 3 a.m. in the midnight; soon she realized it was a nightmare! She was surrounded with anxiety, fear, and powerlessness.

It was another day! Sunlight-soaked curtains were flying in the wind while Amma was engrossed in regular household activities, but Siya wasn't still up. Siya's mother called out to her in between dusting sofa of the drawing room. Kanna, it is twelve in the afternoon; you already missed the dance class; get up now! Her voice got unnoticed yet again, followed by a pin-drop silence. Nobody could understand this silence better than Amma, after not getting any reply for a while; she walked right inside Siya's room and found her half asleep! She sat near her and found she was not well; nah, she was not sick but disturbed! It was her gestures that her mother noticed—ones she had been picking since her childhood days. She was sweaty and cold at the same time. Siya woke up as she felt her mother's touch on her palm.

'Siya, are you not fine?' Amma probed.

'I'm fine, Amma,' Siya said in a sleepy voice.

'No, you're not; I can sense it, Kanna,' declared a worried mother!

'Tell me what is bothering you. It is the first time in ten years that you missed your dance class, and you are telling me you are okay? I object that! Now, please tell me what it is.'

'Will you answer honestly?' asked Siya. 'Of course, Kanna,' Siya's mother replied in a soft, tender voice.

'Am I not beautiful, Amma?'

Amma was terrified by her question, after a minute, she replied, 'You are very pretty, Kanna! Who said you are not beautiful?'

Siya: 'You said you would reply honestly?'

'I said the truth, my love.' Amma consoled.

'Then why do they call me ugly? Is it a curse to be brown and fat?' Amma was in a state of pain after hearing such words from her daughter.

Siya: 'I want to make my own identity, Amma, but society does not accept me the way I'm.' It was the first time in seventeen years a mother saw her daughter questioning her worth. 'No, Siya, get ready; we are going out.' Siya denied it, but Amma convinced her that she will find answers to all her questions once she visits this place. Siya agreed, and they both left for that significant site.

On their way Siya witnessed a field full of dandelion which reminded her how she used to blow them off in the air in her childhood days after making a mighty wish. How Amma used to hold tinny fingers of little Siya all dolled up in a polka dotted top and shiny skirt while she took her to dance classes, crossing that same aisle in childhood. It was a sight which awarded her instant joy which she experienced after such a long time. This was a surreal nostalgic trip which gave Siya a relief that once she was also carefree like a child.

After a while, Siya's mother claimed, 'We are finally here, Kanna.' It was a garden miles away from Siya's house. Siya saw a group of little girls standing in a row, all pumped up to start their *kathak* practice. After gazing at the view and contemplating for some time, the girl who grabbed her attention was a pretty little miss who seemed to be seven years old to be precise; her hair was brown and curly, and her eyes were big; her cheeks were hot pink like cotton candy; she was slim, sleek, and extremely fair, confidently leading the group with her traditional Indian dance moves, adding grace and poise. Siya's eyes suddenly gathered back their shine; how? That was a breakthrough point for Siya, where she saw an earnest glimpse of herself in a girl who looked totally different in outer appearance yet identical! She was not appearing how Siya used to look from any angle, but she was carrying herself like little Siya. That is when Siya acknowledged that her fair skin and Siya's dark skin was having no difference; it was a moment of realization, as if she found a piece of herself calling back home. Siya looked at her mother as tears were rolling down her cheeks. She said, 'Amma, thank you for answering my question this honestly.' Amma pulled her into a big hug and told her, 'I'm so proud of you, Kanna.' They made their way back home with faces full of joy.

Siya woke up zestfully the next morning and went to her dance practice, which she was doing for her upcoming dance competition, set to happen a week later. She participated in the competition and won it. Siya uploaded her dance video, and those usual comments were dropped on it, but this time Siya stood back and answered them all with conviction and self-belief. To her surprise, she got an offer from a leading brand in Mumbai to be a face for their upcoming campaign featuring "plus-size influencers" honouring Indian skin, followed by a theme "Breaking Stereotypes". A rush of sheer happiness flowed in her blood. Siya rushed to the nearby market and bought a heart-touching present for her Amma. Siya grabbed Amma from behind and put the fresh and heavenly fragmented *Gajra* (a veni made of white Mogra flowers) in her mother's hair and uttered in delight, 'I did it, Amma!' She told Amma about the offer she got an hour ago. Amma joined little Siya as they danced their hearts out with their best moves whilst celebrating Siya's victory that evening.

Wrong mirror **often misguides!**

"True beauty of a flower or human sustains
when it blooms from the inside".

Siya got back to the trail, but there is another little fellow who was in need of being brought back home!

Crossing the highway on the streets of Mumbai, off the right track in awe of yellow and red city lights; he was walking strut putting his little hands in the pocket towards nowhere. He looked wistful and sad unlike his name says "Harsh". Thin and malnourished poor boy, eyes were in hope looking up as if the brightest shining star would fall upon him, making his life full of blessings and indulgence; wishfully to be exactly like that handsome stud he follows like a crazy fan at popular "social networking site." Suddenly a voice came from behind—'*Chotu? Kidhar jaa raha hai?*' ('Chotu? Where are you going?')

His dreamy bubble bursts, and he came back to reality! It was another little boy whom Harsh addresses as his best buddy, "Arjun".

'*Tu jaa mai aata hu.*' ('You go, I will come.') Harsh uttered in a heartbroken voice.

Arjun: 'Ok!' Little boy ran towards a busy street!

Harsh took a U-turn towards the same lane; on his way, the poor boy paused to feed stray dogs from his packet of biscuits (kindness was his greatest virtue) and started walking steadily. Came in view a small tea stall, surrounded with a bunch of people sipping the best hot brew of the day. A middle-aged man crushed some ginger, cardamom and put them in hot water, poured some milk and allowed them to ferment as he stirred well. Harsh looked at his face with sympathy and said, 'Baba, wait. I will serve them.'

'Harsh! Where were you?' asked a middle-aged man who was the only guardian to Harsh. A hard-working and devotional man! His father! The little boy kept on dispensing the hot *kulhad* from one fellow to another as he set his neck down in a sad manner. It was a day full of hustle from gold to night. Harsh served the last tea of the night as his father touched a twenty-rupee note to his forehead and closed the shop as the only person in charge cautiously! 'Did you run away to watch those expensive streets again, Chotu?' Harsh's father asked in a curious tone.

Harsh: 'Baba I look thin and skinny; I want to feel smart and attractive; and I want to be one of them. Maybe then he will notice me and reply to my messages politely.'

Baba: 'Harsh you are just a teenager, I cannot afford those overpriced shoes and the fancy jacket you ask for, we are not one of them, why don't you understand!'

'I wish we grow into one,' replied furry poor little boy.

'Besides, tomorrow is a very important day, we have got the liberty to serve as butlers at Shansi Town Hall for a high-profile event,' said Baba.

'Really?' asked the little boy with an over the moon expression on his face.

'Yes! It is a grand opportunity for us to earn some extra pennies, and you will also get complimentary cuisine!' Harsh's father comforted him in a convincing tone.

They both woke up early in the morning prior as it was a big day! Harsh polished the best and only formal pair of shoes he was gifted by his Baba a year ago.

They ended up at the venue and soon were handed serving trays. Harsh prepared, gathering all his enthusiasm, and started attending to the guests with a big smile on his face. Suddenly, his smile converted into an even bigger one. He was awestruck to see his idol boy sitting in the front row of the venue.

Remember the handsome guy who posted ugly comments on Siya's picture? "Shaan" Harsh started adjusting his tie and brushed his hair with his little fingers. He walked towards Shaan with a tray full of hot tea to make an impression. 'Hello sir?' a little boy said, meanwhile a teenage girl was called out on stage to say a few words about the campaign.

Shaan was shocked to see Siya as a lead face at the launch and threw the tray angrily with his left claw at Harsh!

(Little boy was torn apart as if his life's every aspiration came to an end)

Siya:

"Be Like a Rose"

Oh My Rose!

How you could be so divinely beautiful? Even with the thorns hugging you so tight, you know how to grow your paradise.
You know how to carry both beauty and disguise.

Red colour often represents pitfalls, but your red velvet petals always reflect upsides.

Never lose their innocence, bloom, and shine.

You know how to not get afflicted by your spine, but you shed your light on the thorns and make them also look pretty fine.

When you don't push your thorns away but instead use them to safeguard you from those who try to tear you apart.

Isn't it brave of a heart? Oh, my rose I wish all humans could be this divinely beautiful.

Such a small world! We look at each other through Modern Mirrors and try to fit in there! Isn't it unfair?

Mirror could be social, but haven't we been told all our lives that not everything we see is real? For the Wrong Mirror often misguides!

Beauty of a rose or a human sustains when it blooms from the inside.

Oh, my Rose I wish all humans could be this divinely beautiful!

Siya: 'I learnt it hard way, I want to tell you today. Inner beauty is the real beauty which shines from inside as my name says "Siya". A beautiful woman not only from the outside but also from the inside.'

Siya (Beauty), Harsh (Happiness) and Shaan (Pride) were facing each other as their false mirrors fell to pieces that day. Siya learned the meaning of true beauty; Harsh learned the meaning of true happiness through Siya; and Shaan learned the meaning of dignity through two little teenagers.

*****

Author's Message

Do not minimize your true identity to fit into society's false mirror. Fight back against cyberbullying. It is a serious crime!

12

NIGHTGOWN

Uma Iyer

Nightgown is a very common nightwear clothing amongst ladies across the world, especially in India. More often than not, in rural or semi-urban cities and towns, women use this attire not just during the night but also during the entire day. However, in modest Indian urban societies, women are hesitant to wear it from dawn to dusk, and they never consider leaving their homes in one.

Well! Not me. I belong to another universe of thinking.

Hi! I am Vanaja, a teacher by profession and mother to a fourteen-year-old girl named Megha. I wear my nightgown without hesitation. In fact, that is what I wear at all times at home. That too a simple cotton fabric with typical floral and *bandani* prints, a traditional gown called a maxi. And I don't care about who is bothered or cares about it. Because this is my life and I have the freedom to choose what to wear, where to wear it, and when to wear it, and I don't need anybody's validation for it. I was used to women always staring at me, but the new city and the new society I shifted into took me by surprise.

I remember my first morning in this society. I noticed Swati (as I later came to know her) tiptoeing. No. No. She was running quickly, looking like she was escaping out of the door, which was closing and opening secretly and perilously a few moments ago. And guess what? She was in a nightgown. Wow! I thought. So, the ladies here are just like me! Well, maybe I spoke too soon. I soon realized that this society is full of drama queens.

Swati ran fast from the basement of our building to another. She repeatedly knocked on a door. It opened with the sound of the security chain being opened and slid down from behind. Her friend Riddhima opened it. Swati pushed the door open and barged in, closing the door swiftly.

A shocked Riddhima exclaimed, 'What the hell do you think you are doing?'

A panting Swati replied, pointing to the wall clock, 'You asked me to come urgently; it's 6 o'clock in the morning. I didn't even change my night dress. What if someone sees me like this?'

'Who is going to see you at 6 a.m.? And why are you panting so much?'

'I came through the stairs to escape the CCTV cameras in the lift.'

Swati slumped down on the sofa, looking up at Riddhima, shocked, 'What is this?'

'Ssshhh. Don't shout. I wore this kurti in a hurry. It's neither going down completely nor coming up. Help me!'

Swati watched in shock as she saw Riddhima, wearing a tight kurti, bulging all over. She was standing there, unable to lift her hands up.

'Every day I get late for dropping Rani off at the bus stop. By the time I pack the tiffin, get the kids ready, and change my dress, it gets late. It is so embarrassing.'

That was them. And here I was, working in the kitchen in a hurry, packing tiffin, filling a water bottle for Megha, making coffee on one stove, and whatnot. Shridhar, my husband, who was brushing his teeth, looked at me and then at Megha, smiling. Megha smiled and blew a kiss at him. He, too, kissed her. Father-daughter love!

'Coffee is on the table. I am going down to drop Megha.' I grumbled as I walked to Megha, who was tying her shoelace.

'Ready?'

'Yes, Maa.'

Shridhar came out of the hall, wiping his face.

'You will go down like this, in a gown?'

He looked at me from top to bottom. Megha too. So, he continued.

'No, I mean, in my last six months here, I haven't seen any lady in a gown outside the house. The culture is different here.'

'But I just saw one.' I almost defended myself. But why should I? 'The ladies here come out discreetly in a gown. They are shy about wearing a gown in public but bold enough not to wear anything. How cool!'

Shridhar and Megha laughed loudly and high-fived each other.

I was waiting for the lift outside with Megha when the door opposite mine opened again, this time confidently in one go. Swati stepped out with her son. And now guess what? She was dressed nicely in a strapped top and four-pocket pants. The lift arrived. All four of us entered the lift. I looked at Swati's dress (knowing she was in a nightgown early in the morning). Swati settled her hair looking in the mirror, and through the mirror itself, she looked at me in complete distaste, from top to bottom, as if I had just brought disgrace upon her personally.

'You walk out like this?' she asked, pointing to my outfit.

I said casually, 'Why? Is it permissible to wear a gown only to leave the house at 6 a.m.?'

You should have seen the shock on her face. Thankfully, the lift arrived, and she rushed out in a hurry, tugging her son along.

The bus arrived (our kids were in the same school and on the same school bus). After Megha boarded it and left, I turned to head back to my house. But what a sight it was! I stopped in my tracks, shocked. All the ladies gathered downstairs were staring at me. They didn't say anything, but I understood that it was because of my gown. I am good at ignoring and chose to walk away, but not before looking back at Swati, who looked at me and turned away her face to hide.

Days and weeks passed like this. As Shridhar and I took our morning walks together, the ladies looked on, surprised and gossiped.

'My God, just look at this. She's out for a morning walk in a gown, and her husband has no reservations.'

'He must love her a lot. Do you think our husbands would allow this? They couldn't accept our pregnancy and postpartum weight gain.'

'Acceptance, baby, acceptance. Either accept people the way they are or accept life the way it is. It's simple and straight. Just like a gown.'

The ladies laughed at the satire. But we could eavesdrop on some of it.

'My God! Sridhar, so much hesitance and discussion just because of a nightgown.'

'Not everybody is like you, Vanaja. You don't give a damn. Others do.'

But life merges lives. And the connecting thread was our kids. Megha became friends with most of the other kids her age, especially Rani, the famous latecomer Riddhima's daughter. And then one day, the doorbell rang. I opened it to find a reluctant Riddhima and a happy Rani standing outside. I smiled at Rani.

'Hi, Rani.'

'Hello, Aunty. Is Megha there? I was absent today at school, and I need the notes.'

I looked at Riddhima, putting effort into trying to smile. I smiled and nodded at them.

'Yes, please come in.'

I called upon Megha, and she happily took Rani inside, leaving Riddhima feeling lost with me.

'Actually, Rani got her period today and was in severe pain, so she couldn't go to school. She told me Megha is her best friend, so we had to come,' Riddhima said just to start a conversation.

'No problem,' I replied casually. 'Would you like to have some coffee?'

'No, thanks,' was her immediate response. No. Wait. Maybe she didn't want to have coffee made by someone wearing a gown. Right! But I kept calm and started to make coffee anyhow.

'Nice house. Nice interiors,' said Riddhima.

'Thanks. Shridhar—I mean, my husband—is an interior decorator. Mostly, it's his ideas. Simple, sorted. I have no knowledge of presentation in any aspect of life.'

I am sure I heard Riddhima mumbling to herself. 'Just like your dressing.'

I handed the coffee to Riddhima in a steel glass. Riddhima found it difficult to hold it.

'Sorry, we are used to ceramic cups, not steel cups.'

I understood her taunt on status (maybe), then took the cup back and said, 'Oh, sorry, out of habit. We always drink out of steel cups.'

Riddhima asked after a pause.

'We see you going out daily in the mornings. Where do you work?'

'I work with a nearby school here. It is run by the local municipal corporation. It's only for five hours daily. So, I am able to return home before Megha does. You could call it social work.'

'If you are a qualified teacher, you could have joined some private schools here; they pay you better.'

She spoke honestly about this. So, I had to smile.

'No dear. I could never get the same level of satisfaction from teaching children in a private school. I am not working for money. And it's preferable to sitting at home and wasting the entire day.'

Her smile was genuine. Her next question was too

'If you don't mind, can I ask you something?'

'Hmmm.'

'Why are you always in a gown? especially these cotton ones. Nobody wears them here, especially not during the day. Don't you feel uncomfortable? You also came downstairs in these, right? Like...'

'What is the problem with a gown? I don't see any problem with it. In fact, we have been used to it since our childhood days. Maybe because of climate, comfort, or whatever, what better than a cotton gown to keep you cool?'

'Agreed, but throughout the day?'

'Yes, why? We all need comfort the whole day.'

She smiled—a little convinced, a little confused. So, I changed the topic.

'So, what do you do?'

'As of now, work from home. Since the time the lockdown occurred, I am working from home. Freelancing. I had a baby boy last year, and to look after two kids, I need to be home because my husband is mostly away working.'

'In that case, you should always wear a gown because it saves you so much time in choosing, wearing, and changing clothes when you have to multitask so much.'

'I agree. No doubt. I used to wear my gown all the time when I was with my mom after Rani's birth. But here things are different. They expect us to carry ourselves in a certain way. I was also wearing a gown when I came here, but then. Seriously, I waste so much time changing clothes to go down and then changing again at home that I decided to wear a proper dress all day; after all, working and video calling requires that I be properly dressed.'

'But why do you have to change to come down? This is our society. People should know and accept us the way we are.'

She looked at me to speak more.

'People are different, so their points of view will be different. But the choice is ours. Freedom is ours. Options are ours.'

We became friends. And then she introduced me to the entire ladies' gang. They all started liking me slowly, though Swati took more time and coffee to accept me. I even started joining them for morning walks on weekends, in my gown, of course.

Things were going well until Shreeja, my best friend, appeared unexpectedly one day while we were all waiting for the school bus to return with our children. And the moment she saw me, all hell broke loose.

'What the hell do you think you are doing? You are still endorsing the nightgown?'

'I am always endorsing, but no one is getting convinced.'

'But how can you still be the same in a city like this? Unbelievable! She looked at the ladies nervously.'

'If I had to change myself with every city I shifted, then just imagine...' I could only laugh and shrug off her comments. I introduced Shreeja to everyone, and Shreeja was quite shocked by how receptive the ladies were towards me in a gown. Riddhima noticed it and intervened.

'I must say Shreeja. Vanaja is an example. We could never have the kind of confidence Vanaja shows in carrying herself in a gown. I don't think we'll dare to go downstairs in our nightgowns.'

I opened my mouth to say something, but Shreeja cut me off: 'Vanaja, you come downstairs in a gown? Do you even know what you are doing?'

This time I couldn't stop myself from expressing my strong inner beliefs.

'Chill yaar! You guys wear t-shirts, three-fourths, hosiery pants, and track pants at night and come down in them in the mornings. What is it? Nightwear. But western nightwear. I am coming down in

Indian nightwear. What's wrong with it? Why should I put on a different outfit just to go downstairs? And besides, how in the hell do you guys get the time to change in the morning, with so much to do and so much to get ready? We don't even get the time to leisurely use the washroom; we have to wait for the kids to go to even have a bath. I can't change like that. And besides, I don't like anything that is pant-type. "I don't like" means "I don't like." I am comfortable in a gown or skirt while going out. So? Big deal? I hate the rashes and irritation that the pants bring with them. You don't get rashes, or you guys don't sweat, or what? I spend half of my salary on intimate area talcum powder. I can't think of anything else other than a cotton maxi. And look at you! In which clothes are you guys actually happy? You can't wear sleeveless or half-pants without first waxing. You wear an *anarkali* just to hide your tummy. I can't even understand how you ladies fit yourselves into and get out of such tight-fitting dresses and leggings. When the pants are pulled out, they always come out in the opposite direction, one on the correct side and one on the wrong side. I can do my entire housework in my simple outfit in the time you spend sitting, pulling them on you, and getting rid of them. My gown has pockets to stuff my phone and keys. I have to dry only one piece of cloth, which helps in the monsoon. And besides, gowns are universal. We can donate them to the needy without thinking twice, like when a calamity strikes, because we know they can fit any lady. Having a stock on hand is always beneficial. And the so-called "gown dress", which is currently fashionable. It's just a stand-in for my gown styles.'

Well, that day I felt like I had given a Ted-X talk on women's power and the freedom to wear what we choose. I did expect the kind of applause that Akshay Kumar got after his talk at the climax of the movie Padman. But alas!

And. Now...

Riddhima is working from home in a gown. The client (a woman) is a US client. A video call is going on. The client asks Riddhima,

'Hi. I want to ask you something.'

'Yes.'

'What are you wearing?'

'Why? What happened? Something wrong?'

'No! Nothing wrong. It is so colourful. I love the print.'

Riddhima smiles.

'So, what is it? Can you stand up and show me?'

Riddhima pauses, thinks, stands up confidently, and says, 'It's an Indian outfit. We call it a maxi gown. It is supposed to be a nightgown, but because of its comfort, we prefer it during the daytime too at home.'

'Doesn't matter what you wear; your work is more important. Just between me and you. Off the records. Can I ask something again?'

'Yes.'

'I'll give you my address; can you send a few of these to me?'

Riddhima laughed. 'Sure, my pleasure.'

And today, as I serve coffee to all my friends in my steel cups, I am happy. Not only because I finally persuaded everyone to support my maxi concept, but also because it demonstrated how women are succumbing to society's (non-existent) demands and transforming themselves into something they are not. I am happy for the freedom, both for myself and for them.

It was time for a party. In a maxi…

*****

Author's Message

Every person has the right to wear what they like and feel comfortable in, even if it is looked down upon by others.

13

A SECOND HELPING

Tulsi Nambiar

The dining table was surrounded by people eager to be around each other. The air was overflowing with excitement in anticipation of the meal, which soon lay before us. But I did not share the common feeling; instead, I sat silently in my seat, staring at my empty plate, wishing I did not have to be here. I was apprehensive about having to eat, and I wondered if I could avoid it. But I knew that was not a viable option. With avid reluctance, I served myself enough rice to be seen and enough to keep me sane. On it, I poured the thick, yellowish-brown gravy, in which some pieces of the tender chicken swam. I took my seat, dreading the process of actually having to eat what was on my plate.

Before beginning, I waited for everyone else at the table to serve themselves. I nibbled unhurriedly at the scarce amount that seemed like a mountainous amount to my meddling brain. I prayed hard, hoping that my companions wouldn't notice the amount of food on my plate and that I would be spared any harsh judgement.

I listened to their joyous bursts of laughter, and I could make out the cracks in their voices as they retold nostalgic stories that come around at every meal repeatedly; we all knew them off by heart. In a trice, I felt eyes glued to me, and my heart started to thump louder than an elephant's stomp against my fragile ribcage, expecting a sarcastic comment about me. I was so conscious of myself when I was alone, and even more so when I was around people. I believed in the fact that everyone noticed me and would immediately come to a negative conclusion about my appearance.

I nibbled again, despising myself for reaching a stage where food made me want to curl up. I dug myself a grave underground because it caused such an extreme level of fear. In the distance, I heard my niece scream and shout because she did not want to eat, and eventually her mother let her be. I wished I was five again, so I could avoid eating with such ease and no one would question me as to why I did not want to eat. The idea of eating had become the biggest task of my day. I was struggling to sit at a table where everyone was eating lump-sum amounts of food, and they did not grapple with every mouthful but were quick to stuff themselves with more. I was nearly envious.

I looked down at my plate and the amount I began with remained. I closed my eyes, hoping that as I opened them again, the food on my plate would have magically vanished, but sadly, that was not how reality worked. I squinted at my plate, and my wish had not come true. I sat with my shoulders slumped as I tried to swallow the morsel of food lurking at the back of my throat.

I refilled myself with another mouthful, or a mouthful and a half. My heart jumped, and as I tasted the many flavours in my mouth, I felt a rush of desire for the amount of food that lay on my plate. My mind was racing faster than the pace of my chewing, and I could feel my heart beating out of my chest. Every part of my body wanted me to eat more, to eat the brightly coloured, brightly coated chicken with the dusky rice with brick-red eyes on each grain. There were these rare occasions when I ate that I felt this way, and I fought with myself, fought with that villainous thought of wanting more. How dare my body even think about wanting more? Especially when I was around other people, what if they noticed a sudden change in my body?

I shut my thoughts down. My fingers mechanically made a ball out of the rice and placed it in my mouth; my tongue swirled around it, yearning for the flavour. But my teeth quickly chewed, taking away the opportunity. I was left with just the tasteless crumbs of rice sitting on my tongue; the desire to eat had been successfully eliminated. I had become an expert at doing so. I kept pecking at the food that my brain had decided to dislike.

My attention went to a time, only a few months ago, when I could eat as much as the others around me with no difficulty, carefree of its impact. But today, I was fighting my own mind to eat what little I was eating, and I was purposefully preventing myself from eating more. I had learned to convince myself that the inadequate amount I ate was sufficient, even when my body gave me signals to say otherwise. My mind had managed to turn food, my only comfort, into something that should repulse me. The opinions of everyone around me were ingrained in my brain, which did not allow me to eat. It was an attempt to meet the expectations people had of me.

My intestines opened up, and as I continued to push little food down, my stomach grumbled in acknowledgement of the food it was receiving. I looked around, waiting for a reaction from the others around me, but they were all in oblivion. I rubbed my stomach, hoping to reduce if not stop the sounds it was making, but instead, I felt bloated, and paranoia struck harder than ever before. I became aware. I became conscious. My mind started ticking. I wanted to stop eating that very second and starve myself for the rest of the day. I knew it was not a plausible plan, but there was nothing wrong with at least devising it in my mind. I again peeked above my plate; everyone was filling their mouths with more and more food, grinning with pleasure. I had the urge to tell them to stop. How can they eat so much and still remain in good shape? It isn't fair that I used to do the same as they did, but my shape changed—a shape that I loathed.

I forcefully stuffed my mouth with some more food, which lay on my plate in abundance. I examined the quantity of food on my plate, and I looked at the large dishes at the centre of the table with a hundred times the amount I was eating. I could feel eyes watching me for a second time, this time with purpose. I looked to my side to find him looking at me with sympathy in his eyes. I tried to avoid looking at him directly, but I knew he had noticed my grapple and would not leave me easily. He pressed his hand against my thigh, hoping that would encourage me to eat calmly. I hated myself for needing a physical stimulus to eat, but fortunately or unfortunately, it did not provoke me to eat. Instead, I went on thinking about the events that would take place after I managed to eat.

He knew as soon as I would finish my meal, I would complain, saying, 'I'm hungry even though I actually ate.' And he would always respond by saying, 'It's because you barely ate; you need to eat more,' before offering more food, which I denied without fail. It is the same line everyone around me, who noticed my eating, said to me, 'You need to eat more.' But I cannot. I had reached a place where hunger lingered in me throughout the day, but I could not bring myself to eat.

I glared at the food on my plate because it was testing the limits of my brain. My breathing quickened. I tried shutting my eyes, hoping that the darkness would help me forget food and eating. As the skulking paranoia knocked from the back of my mind, I could feel the desire to stop eating grow stronger. It was silly, but I was so sure that every little morsel of food was affecting my body negatively. The paranoia was taking over.

I opened my eyes, and he was still looking at me, imploring me to eat. I tried to take a few deep breaths, but I'd had enough. I pushed my chair back and rushed out of the room. I needed to measure the change in my body. I ran away with purpose. I ran to the nearest weighing scale in the house and measured myself. I was confident that I had gotten bigger from the half meal; I had eaten in the past sixteen hours. I looked down at the number through eyes as blurry as a windscreen on a stormy day; the number had not changed from an hour ago.

I was certain that the scale was wrong; I ate, and you saw me, didn't you? How could it not show? My mind was not sane enough to comprehend the way science worked or even how my body worked. I paced the room, anxious as if my stillness would lead to a change in the number that would show on the scale. I breathed again, hoping that my anxiety would cease.

In my chest, I felt the few mouths of food I had gathered and assembled. At that moment, I wished I could puke and be free of everything external inside of me. The flavour of the chicken rolled on my tongue, pushing me to go and eat. But my mind forced my feet to remain immobile. I closed my eyes, and the image of the plate I left behind revealed itself. Clearly, I had not reached a point where I could eat at social gatherings; my anxiety was not willing to let it go, not even once.

It was indisputable that I was losing my mind; I was going crazy—all because I was determined to look a certain way. In the process of getting there, I was willing to give up on my mental health; I was unconcerned about how erratically I was behaving. I wanted to be thin because that was what was perfect, no matter what else I had to give up to reach my goal.

He walked in, interrupting my thoughts, but what I saw in his hands angered me. He came in with my plate of food that I had left behind. 'Eat.' I shook my head vigorously. 'How much longer? How many more days, weeks, and months will it take for you to realize that you need to eat?' I stared at him blankly. He came closer, hoping to touch me and hand me the plate. I stood expressionless and motionless until he gave up, and he did because I was more stubborn than him.

He was new to this; he was not entirely sure how to help me. I did not want his help, which he was unwilling to understand. He often told me, 'You look fine' or 'I never really noticed.' But he was lying to me; I could see it in his eyes. He did notice how my clothes had become baggier on me; he did notice how my cheeks stuck to me more; and he did notice how my fingers had become bony. How could he not notice such changes? Were they not big enough to be noticed? My mind raced again. Had my body not changed after all? Was I starving myself for no reason? A million thoughts clouded my head and sight.

Suddenly, everything around me turned black, and I could feel my legs give way from under me. Literally, paranoia had finally taken a toll on my body. I collapsed on the mosaic flooring, leaving behind all my worries. I was instantly free of thoughts, and the darkness took over me.

A bang on the table brought me back to reality—a reality that is quite different. Today, I sat with the same people I did a few months ago, and my old grapple overeating has almost disappeared. I pierced my fork and twirled around the saucy spaghetti covered in cheese and herbs; the smell of garlic and mushrooms intoxicated my nose; and I stuffed my mouth in the same way as everyone else around me.

I joined their bursts of laughter with my own and told parts of the nostalgic stories that came around again. I smiled as they stuffed their mouths, knowing that I was doing the same, unlike last time. I looked to my side, grateful that he had returned for me that day, only to find me unconscious on the floor. I remember him saying, 'I told you; you need to eat.' I remember how I cried in pain, both physically and emotionally.

'Can I give you a second helping?' he asked.

Anxiety bubbled in me. Yes, I had started to eat after the little fiasco, but I had yet to start taking seconds. He served my plate with just a little, knowing very well where my brain was heading. I could feel his hand around my shoulder, and he smiled with pride.

I looked at him and then at my food, and I looked at him and then at my plate. I glanced his way one last time and then focused on my food.

I looked at the white spaghetti from which smoke evaporated; the urge to resist was growing, and old habits were making it known. My heart beat steadily as I contemplated how much this would affect me. I looked at him again, fear written on my face. He simply said, 'You can eat.' I took a deep breath.

If I consume what is on my plate, it is not a crime; I am allowed seconds, and I am allowed the extra space on Earth that it may cause. I need to eat. I have to eat. I can eat. I want to eat. The stereotypical body shape expected by society was not worth starving myself for. The societal expectation of me, which claimed, I must look and be a certain size as a female, was not worth me warding off food forever.

Slowly and meticulously, I began to slurp the rolled pasta off my fork. I chewed, relishing the different flavours that diffused on my tongue. I closed my eyes and swallowed the morsel with ease. Every mouthful felt like an achievement; every mouthful was a sign I was getting better. I held his hand, gathering the strength to continue, to push away the thought telling me to stop. I put the last strand of spaghetti in my mouth; it almost felt ceremonious. I sat back, satisfied with the meal but more with myself. I smiled at him. The others looked at me, unsure of what made me feel so joyful. They were completely unaware of how significant this moment was for me. I finally had a successful meal after so many months. Can you believe it? I ate; I had seconds too, and I pushed away the deranged thoughts and ate.

*****

Author's Message

In my own life, I have taken steps towards fighting the image and expectation of a perfect body. This, I think, is the genesis of acceptance.

14

THE GIRL WITH A DREAM

Irene Munyiri

Over the years, women have been degraded and treated as second-class citizens. They always had to fight long and hard to be heard and included. It may sound cliché at this point because it may seem like they have already achieved much. But the truth is that there are women who are still fighting to be heard and women who are still fighting to be included. Women of colour have to fight extra hard to be included because they are, sadly, fighting two battles: one for being heard and another against discrimination due to their skin colour. Women face numerous barriers in society that prevent them from achieving their goals. Early marriage is a particularly big problem, especially for girls who come from conventional families. It is sad when the dreams of these girls are ignored and remain just that—dreams.

This is the story of a woman who is still fighting with the hope that one day she will be heard and allowed to take part in things that really matter. She was born in the late 1900s, which means that she was born in an era where women had a place at the table. This was, however, not the case for her. She was brought up by a misogynistic father and a woman who believed that she and every other woman's place was in the kitchen. A reason for this attitude is the high rate of illiteracy among Africans, as most illiterate people still hold on to the old beliefs of their forefathers. Not just the illiterate, but even the literate ones still insist on following the ways of the people who came before them. Some of these practices are harmful and have a negative effect on people. It is a harsh reality that some beings fail to realize how backwards some of these practices are—so backwards that a society cannot even grow because they bring the past into the future.

She was the firstborn daughter in a family of five. Her mother raised her and her sisters to serve. She taught them to shrink themselves and their personalities in order to accommodate other people. She taught them to be wives and mothers. She was raised to take orders from people who often treated her as a lesser being, and being raised like that, she saw no problem in it. Instead, she took pride in serving people because she was always very passionate about whatever she did, no matter how small it was. Sadly, this was not what was taught to the boys. The boys were taught to be strong, to believe in their dreams, and not to settle for anything but the best. The "men" in the family were taught to be vibrant and confident. They were raised with the ideology that they should sit and bark orders; after all, women were there at their beck and call. Their parents did not consider that in the twenty-first century, both women and men go to work. Women have careers, as opposed to medieval times when women would stay at home, cook, clean, and care for the family. Things were changing, and they refused to acknowledge that.

She joined the school and was very excited about it; she used to emerge as the top student in her class at all times. She loved the Queen's English; it would speak to her in a way that her first language never did. She improved her writing and expressed herself better, and she gained confidence that had not been instilled in her as a child. The school was not easy for her; she had to be her own cheerleading squad because her parents didn't care. She constantly had panic attacks, and she constantly had moments when she didn't believe in herself. It was at this moment that she would feel frustrated and constantly ask herself, 'All this is for what? What if I fail? What if destiny does not favour my success?' She had so many "what if" questions in her mind all the time. This was only natural because she felt drained; she no longer had the zeal to work hard to achieve her dreams.

But, in spite of all the doubts she had, she still rose; she still kept some fighting spirit alive in herself.

True to the words of Malcolm Forbes, her perspective changed, and she started to view things differently. Mirrors and windows were undoubtedly turned. She wanted the world; she wanted to be like Condoleezza Rice; she wanted to break the glass ceiling. She no longer wanted to be the little naive girl who would be trampled upon by people; she wanted to command respect and be heard. How could she then change her parents' perceptions of what a girl should be? How could she convince her misogynistic father that she could be more, that she could achieve the same success as boys and men, or even better? As she grew, she experienced a lot of challenges, and her parents, as you might guess, were of little or no help. She, on the other hand, did not back down; she knew what she wanted and was determined to achieve it, come rain or shine.

Despite hailing from a misogynistic father, he still gave her an education, not because he knew she needed it but because the government advocated for it. In the eyes of her father, she was a woman who would be married off someday to start her own family. She did not let that stop her because she knew that if she got an education, she would run away to go and achieve her dreams; she would elope with her dreams and let destiny decide what would become of her. All she knew was that she was not meant for the typical life of an African woman—to get married, give birth to children, take care of her husband, and later on die without having achieved anything and without making a name for herself. Her childhood difficulties did not break her spirit or soul. Rather, they fuelled her desire to become a better woman, a woman who would be a torchbearer for other women like her and a woman who would lead other women like herself to the biblical Canaan for women.

When she reached the legal age to drive and even after getting her permit, her father would not allow her to drive because it was not a "woman's thing". He would always let her brothers, who were younger than her, take the wheel. This made her feel a little bit worthless because her dream was always to hit the open road with her windows rolled down, listening to her favourite band as the warm African breeze went through her typical 4C hair. This broke her, but she did not let it destroy her zeal. She believed that one day she would own her car and drive it wherever her heart desired. Her zeal and determination were second to none, and, just like the wind, she decided that the direction of her life would not be determined by anybody. She was not willing to give away that power; that was her superpower, and she promised herself that she would guard it with her life. She was more than willing to go above and beyond to get the things she knew she deserved.

When she got to the university, things became thick for her. Her father was no longer willing to educate her. After all, why does a woman need all that education? It would only make her wayward and stubborn. It would make it difficult for her to be a "submissive wife" to her husband. The father had seen her fighting spirit, and he knew that education would liberate her; he knew that she would soar high with a degree in her hands, making her unstoppable. She got admission to one of the best universities in her country, but her heart immediately broke when she saw the letter. Success was well within her reach, but financial constraints were hunting her like a dog. She did not know what to do because she did not want to start her life with crippling student loans. She wanted to start her life with a clean slate. She still had the same warrior spirit within her.

This was when she decided to go back to the drawing board. She was determined to get an education; after all, education is the key to success. She tried to observe all the options she had without having to take out student loans. All her efforts to look for a way out were futile; she had two options: either get a job or take a student loan. She had never been in such a difficult situation before. She felt that whatever decision she made could go either way. She weighed her options. If she decided to get a job, it would become extremely difficult for her to concentrate fully on her studies because, to raise enough money for her school, she would have to take on two, three, or even more jobs and try to get overtime gigs to make ends meet. She needed money for upkeep, rent, and school. She eventually made a tough decision: she decided to get a job. How hard could it be? Other people had done it and succeeded, so she knew she was not a lesser being and could do it too. She could handle the pressure. She had the burning desire to do the impossible. Doing hard things was her identity, or was it?

She started applying for jobs everywhere. She sent her application to companies of every sector—restaurants, factories, bars, casinos, nightclubs, you name it—as long as they were hiring, she would apply. She waited for a couple of months before getting any response. Her patience began to wear thin, and she lost all hope, especially after looking at her peers, who had already been admitted and were going on with their classes. Every post on Facebook, Instagram, and Snapchat of her peers at the university enjoying their lives reminded her of her misfortunes. She eventually got a call back from a factory; it was a little far from her university and the pay was not as good as she thought it would be, but as long as there was cash coming in at the end of the month, she was willing to take the job. She was optimistic, as she was always very passionate about everything, she set her mind to. She took as many overtime opportunities as she could. This really exhausted her, and by the time she had her classes, she was too tired to even concentrate. She often forgot to hand in assignments, or when she did, she handed them in late and incomplete. Her lecturers became impatient with her; her scores were poor, and she barely made it to class on time.

As much as she needed the money to survive and pay her school fees, she was not willing to stand by and watch all her dreams go down the drain. The goal was to get a good education and a great GPA; she was not willing to take anything less. She had worked too hard to reach where she already was. She knew that she had to prove her father and society wrong. And, in addition to proving society wrong, she was doing it for herself, her sisters, and all the other women in her society who looked up to her. She decided to fix her crown, re-strategize, take control of her life, and achieve everything she always wanted to. She asked herself, 'What would Condoleezza do?'

She decided to take an academic break from school for a year just so that she could find her footing. She needed to get back on track. She stopped competing with her peers and realized that her journey was different from theirs. She no longer wanted to have a picture-perfect life for Instagram, TikTok, and Snapchat; she wanted the real deal; she wanted to succeed on her own terms. During her time off of school, she learned to manage her time, organize her work in order to prevent burnout and juggle many activities at once in order to avoid anxiety. She learned to be self-reliant, beat deadlines, and practice the virtue of discipline. She started to journal out her feelings, where she wanted to be, and how far she had come. This was a growing season for her. She did not want to go back to school and mess up the same way she did the first time. She knew that society does not give girls like her a second chance; she knew that the world was unfair, and in order to get what she wanted, she had to reach out and grab it, as no one would hand it to her on a silver platter.

When one year had lapsed, she eventually went back to school, more determined than ever. She attended all her classes on time, and she was able to do her assignments diligently and hand them in on time. Soon she became a favourite of her lecturers. Her GPA shot up in no time. Indeed, no human being is limited. She actively participated in the class. She easily became one of the best and brightest students the university had ever had. She, on the other hand, did not let her university's "fame" get to her head; she was only concerned with one thing: finishing her degree. All this time, she was still juggling between work and school, but this time it seemed more seamless because she was more organized and had her head in the game.

She eventually graduated at the top of her class. That day became one of the happiest days of her life. She overcame and emerged victorious despite the hurtful words of naysayers. When she fell, she did not stay down; she rose and got things done because that is what strong women do—they rise to the occasion and draw on. She got her dream job immediately after, and true to her words, she got a beautiful home in the plush suburbs. She was finally able to afford her dream car. She finally earned the respect she had sought all her life. Even her misogynistic father had changed the way he viewed her. She was looked up to by society, and she became a role model for many. I'm sure if Condoleezza knew her, she would be extremely proud of what she was able to achieve.

Indeed, there is absolutely nothing new under the sun. Whatever we set our minds to can be accomplished, regardless of what society thinks. Women are a force to look out for in the future; they are strong-willed, and they fight for what they deserve. Whatever they put their minds to will eventually materialize. They guard what they believe in with all they have, and they do not relent; that's a virtue everyone should aim to have.

*****

Author's Message

Societal constraints have caused the death of a lot of dreams, especially the dreams of women, because they are viewed and treated differently. It is past time for society to abandon its bias against women and allow women to thrive. Nothing established by a woman easily crumbles. Societies that have given their women a chance have propagated. It is important to note, however, that glass ceilings can be broken, and the sky is no longer the limit.

15

A JUDGED BRAVE KID

Awantika Gupta

At the tender age of four or five, Sasuke's parents moved to a new apartment, and he was an innocent and sweet child who had yet to grasp societal norms. On one occasion, his mother's friend asked him why his mother hadn't called her the previous night. In his innocence, Sasuke replied, 'The telephone bills were so costly, so my mother intentionally didn't call you.' Little did he know that this innocent comment would land him in trouble when he relayed the conversation to his mother. It's quite amusing, isn't it? But it's a true testament to Sasuke's innocence, as what more can one expect from a child?

Learning to coexist naturally with others as he or she grows is more important for a child than acquiring social filters. However, Sasuke's experience was different. Upon moving to Kolkata with his parents, he found himself isolated from his new friends in their new apartment. Despite speaking the same language, sharing the same cuisine, and participating in the same rituals, he felt like an outsider. Living in a small town in West Bengal and transitioning to Kolkata, Sasuke was unaware of how being a Bihari in a Bengali community could significantly impact his life.

According to societal norms, the concept of "judgment" often requires individuals to conform to established standards, which parents often fear for their children. They persistently push their children to become better individuals, fearing that society will not show them respect otherwise. But who exactly is this "society"? Aren't we all part of it? Do we possess the right to pass judgment on others? Sasuke, like any other child, played and made mistakes, exhibiting typical mischievous behaviour. However, he experienced a higher level of judgment compared to his peers. Even his friends and their parents, who were part of the so-called society, passed judgment on him and criticized his cultural background. People never missed an opportunity to remind Sasuke of his roots whenever he made a simple mistake, expressed an opinion, approached someone, or shared stories. Despite this, the incredibly sweet and innocent child continued to consider them his friends and extended family.

Sasuke's parents were well aware of the presence of these unkind individuals and took it upon themselves to teach their beloved child valuable lessons, ensuring that he wouldn't be emotionally affected and could lead a successful life. Upon discovering the harsh realities, Sasuke began disregarding those individuals whom he once considered close. He understood that he had to work hard to prove himself for his own benefit and to remind others of their own shortcomings. These people never missed an opportunity to criticize his school, college, teachers, and even the places he visited with his parents. However, Sasuke didn't learn to filter his actions and words merely to impress society; instead, he chose to cultivate inner calmness and prioritize engagement in his own life.

While Sasuke undoubtedly had some pleasant memories with his friends and was surrounded by people, it wasn't the aspect of his life that he treasured the most. Despite all the challenges he faced, he managed to excel in school and was happy with his school life. School is a unique space where we learn about various emotions like love, care, crushes, and invaluable life lessons. Throughout his thirty years of life, Sasuke experienced numerous phases, including romantic relationships, break-ups, significant and minor accidents, job scarcity, job insecurity, low income, survival, and loneliness.

Sasuke, driven by his own principles and passions, lived life on his own terms, unaffected by the judgments of others. However, during his early teenage years, a time when dreams and imaginings hold significant sway, he found himself slightly adrift. Sasuke, who often found himself lost in deep thinking, would frequently get caught up in the twists and turns of his own thoughts. As he navigated the complexities of youth and explored his romantic inclinations, he also grappled with the need to focus on his career, resulting in a clash of priorities. Emotionally, he was pulled in various directions—balancing his love life, the pursuit of a suitable job, parental expectations, and the ever-present barrier of judgment from society. At times, Sasuke recognized his own mistakes, yet he struggled to exert control over his actions.

It wasn't Sasuke's fault at all, as the youth phase is often seen as a time of exploration where we all make mistakes. Sasuke was no different from the rest of us. There are times when he longs for his childhood, especially when his father used to teach him every evening. Despite coming home tired from work, his father dedicated himself to teaching Sasuke without wasting any time. Sasuke's parents wanted to provide him with every happiness in life, but sometimes they unintentionally imposed judgment on him. They placed a lot of pressure on Sasuke and often compared him to other children in the community, much like many other parents do.

Sasuke had an exceptional memory and vividly recalled the time when his father received a promotion and began commuting to work by car. Suddenly, his father's social standing and reputation improved in the eyes of society. However, Sasuke couldn't forget the harsh memories he had experienced. From an early age, he learned the important lesson of continuously striving to prove himself, ensuring that no one would have the opportunity to humiliate him again.

When children are pressured to live up to societal expectations, it can be a heavy burden for them. Why should kids be raised solely based on society's demands? It leaves them unable to find peace in their sleep or tranquilly in their thoughts. Additionally, children often rely on sharing their thoughts with siblings or close friends, but Sasuke didn't have anyone like that. Being an only child, Sasuke felt like he was building a world of loneliness in his own mind, even amidst his family, friends, school, and all the fun around him.

During that time, Sasuke may not have been fully aware of the impact of his isolation from society on his attitude and mental state, but he found solace and contentment within himself. His deepest affection was reserved for his maternal grandparents, with whom he shared a special bond. Sasuke's grandmother lovingly prepared his favourite meals, and his maternal grandfather took him on walks and played with him, creating cherished memories together. One day, Sasuke's mother grew concerned when he didn't return home after playing outside for an extended period. When he finally came back, Sasuke explained that he had been wandering alone in a nearby field, lost in his thoughts. It was intriguing to see a young child exploring the vastness of the field, deep in contemplation, at such an innocent age. One couldn't help but wonder what was going on in his young mind during that time.

It's true that in this story, we may have found ourselves passing judgment on Sasuke. However, I must acknowledge any mistakes I made in delivering the story because Sasuke is far from being an unfortunate child. Despite facing numerous challenges, he is a resilient and determined young boy who refuses to succumb to societal pressures. Sasuke has proven himself to be a remarkable individual who stands a little higher than everyone else, unyielding in his pursuit of success and fulfilment. Even though he did not study at big institutions like IIT and IIM, there was no dearth in his ability. He may not have fulfilled many of the dreams of his mother and father, but the desire in him to know everything and the talent he had shown so far in his life were not ordinary things.

In today's world, many young people tend to procrastinate and evade their responsibilities. However, Sasuke was different. He never learned the habit of procrastination and instead chose to live his life on his own terms. He embraced a different approach to life—one that was characterized by success, passion, vibrancy, and cycling. Though his life was ordinary rather than extravagant, a shift in perspective reveals how Sasuke faced constant judgment from society, his parents, and others. Remarkably, he transformed these judgments into sources of strength. Sasuke proved everyone's judgments wrong and stood confidently against them all.

As a child, Sasuke felt uncomfortable around people who constantly reminded him of his origins. However, today those same individuals praise him for his remarkable success. It's another form of judgment, but a positive one. Although Sasuke performed well academically, he struggled with a recurring issue—he had a tendency to get easily angered and hasn't yet mastered anger management. Regardless of the challenges he faced, he refused to yield to anyone and maintained a relentless attitude towards himself. Unfortunately, this mindset led to several moments of sadness in his life.

When Sasuke began his college journey, he found himself easily distracted and unable to fully focus on his studies. He sought moments of relaxation and enjoyment by making new friends and exploring his romantic interests. Unaware of what lay ahead in his destiny, he embraced the experience of discovering life. However, after college, a significant turning point arrived, forcing him to leave behind everything he knew and venture into a new city. This new destination held uncertain and challenging paths. Without any assistance, he had to forge his own path and create a fulfilling life for himself—one that would be filled with success and fulfilment.

He accepted the challenge but definitely wished that "The God" had alerted him beforehand about all this drama that was waiting for him. Sasuke likes to live his life like a free bird and ignore all the pressure and boundation from society. After getting many warnings to stay tied and silent, he remained free. Just like an eagle, he proved difficult to trap in a net.

During that phase, Sasuke experienced emotional ups and downs, often feeling uncertain. His inability to communicate openly with his family contributed to his initial sense of being lost. Not only was he far away from home, but he was also relocated to a new city. The once cherished child of his parents now found himself in a solitary city where he had no acquaintances. He couldn't reach out to his mother when he was hungry, nor could he ask his father for anything he needed. Memories of his friends brought him comfort in moments of loneliness, but he couldn't physically be with them.

Sasuke was alone, with a multitude of questions swirling in his mind. Despite feeling saddened and weary, he mustered up his strength and embarked on a new journey, pedalling forward on an unfamiliar path.

During that time, Sasuke made two important decisions that became the guiding principles of his life. The first principle was "never to look back", which meant he would value his relationships and fulfil his responsibilities, but he wouldn't hesitate to forge his own path when necessary. The second principle was to live life on his own terms, unwavering and unyielding. Regardless of the challenges he faced, he vowed to maintain his unique lifestyle without compromising his values or disrespecting others.

Sasuke arrived in the new city and experienced nights of hunger. He discovered affordable food options and managed to find a rented hostel. Now, being alone in the city, Sasuke couldn't shake off the numerous questions that plagued his mind. Memories from his childhood constantly resurfaced, and he found himself reflecting on the highs and lows of his entire life. Perhaps the challenges Sasuke faced were a result of his own karma, his father's hard work, his mother's struggles, and the judgments imposed by society.

Sasuke's sorrow remained misunderstood by others. Every memory of his childhood held a tinge of bitterness, and as he grew older, he carried a heavy burden. With a deep love for cycling, Sasuke found solace in riding long distances, spanning hundreds or even thousands of kilometres, to pursue his passion. Perhaps he pushed himself on his bike to overcome the hardships and difficulties he faced.

Today, Sasuke is a successful individual who constantly strives for personal growth and progress. He has taken control of his own destiny and shaped his luck through his efforts. However, he continues to face challenges and obstacles that come with the passage of time. Despite the struggles he faces, Sasuke remains committed to living life on his own terms. While this may have caused some dissatisfaction from his parents, he continues to achieve remarkable accomplishments, which hold greater importance to him.

Even now, life continues to provide Sasuke with diverse experiences that remind him of the critics and judgmental individuals in society. However, he has learned not to let these insignificant matters affect him. He has grown indifferent to the opinions of others, focusing instead on what truly matters to him and finding fulfilment in his own path.

Today, Sasuke finds himself in a position of knowledge and continuous growth. He upholds discipline in his life and is passionate about fitness and finding joy and contentment within his own world. His parents have provided him with a solid education, nurturing his courage and character. However, it remains a challenge for others to truly grasp the essence of who he is as a person and as a human being.

Sasuke went through numerous moments of self-loss and distance from his loved ones. Only he truly comprehended the depths of his pain. In this new city, he sought solace in making new friends and joining various groups. While he enjoyed weekend relaxation after a five-day job, he gradually began to realize that these activities did not bring him genuine happiness.

Real happiness requires genuine efforts. Sasuke prioritizes self-care and consciously chooses the path that aligns with his values. However, there is a deeper reason behind his unwavering commitment to staying on the right path. Sasuke had a terrible accident that could have cost him his life. It was a wake-up call for him, making him realize that if he had died, his life would have been in vain. Recognizing this second chance given by fate, he understands the importance of making the most of it. Sasuke feels the need to constantly prove himself and make each moment count in his life.

Sasuke sees himself as an eagle, fearlessly soaring above storms and taking leaps of faith with great courage. Additionally, he admires the principle of wolves, who remain focused and alert in every step of life. These powerful symbols inspire him to approach life with bravery, resilience, and a keen sense of awareness.

Fuelled by strength and courage, Sasuke confidently pedals both the wheels of his bicycle and the wheel of his life. Material wealth holds no importance to him; his focus lies on making a meaningful impact. He carries no negativity within him and considers himself somewhat extraordinary, yet he embraces the courage to transform his ordinary life into something remarkable.

Sasuke has outgrown the burden of judgments, caste, and his roots. Today, his sole focus is on his abilities and the outcomes he can achieve. Sasuke is committed to "keep grinding" with someone in his life to maintain a harmonious and fulfilling journey.

*****

Author's Message

Life has two wheels: one that moves you forward and one that pulls you back. Make deliberate choices about your life's direction and have confidence in yourself.

16

LITTLE ACTS OF HOPE

Vaishnavi. S

Even a small action of ours can make a significant difference in someone's life. All it takes is having the mental capacity to help another person and prioritizing him or her over us for a while. As a social worker, I was fortunate enough to have a job that let me do what I always wanted to do: be there for others when they really needed it. I got the opportunity to serve homeless people with mental illness.

The human brain is enigmatic by nature, even with all the advanced technologies. The way people think, and their consequent actions are always mysterious. There are a number of mental illnesses and disorders that affect people, and most often, it's difficult to pinpoint the exact reason for their occurrence. This is one of the reasons that the study of the human brain and its functions, in addition to human behaviour, is both an interesting and difficult field of study.

Most of us enjoy travelling and discovering new places and people, as well as learning about our lives and adventures. Everyone has unique and interesting stories to share. There are also people who remain a constant fixture on our streets but always go unnoticed. Nobody does it purposefully; it's just that people don't see what they are not looking for, "the obvious unseen". These are the homeless and those who rely on begging for a living. We never bother to even look at them, but they are living in society while being blatantly ignored. We never care whether they have food three times a day, whether the food that they consume is clean, or where they stay. The fact is that, even though there is nothing certain in their lives, they manage to survive with what little they have; most often, people are willing to help them by buying them food and helping them with money.

When it comes to homeless people with mental illness, things become more difficult. People mostly consider them a threat, as they think that these people can be unpredictable and violent, but that's not always true. The truth is that our human brain consists of several kinds of chemicals that perform unique functions. A slight variation in the brain chemicals can lead to multiple problems, and this is the case in people with mental illness, accompanied by different social factors as well. The changes happening in the brain are mostly treatable with timely and proper support. People with mental illness can also lead a very happy life, but because of people's misconceptions, beliefs, and stigma, they often end up not getting adequate support. And as time goes on, the person himself or herself as well as his or her family will find it difficult to manage the issues arising because of his or her illness or condition. All these issues can lead to the family abandoning the person with mental illness or to the person himself or herself wandering away from his or her home. There are many reasons why a person with mental illness becomes homeless. Sometimes the family must have found professional help for such people, but they don't take their medicines regularly and see no improvement. When this pattern continues, after a certain point in time, the family will give up hope, and eventually, the person will become homeless.

I would like to share a story about a person who got lost not because of his fault but because of things that were beyond his control.

I used to work as a social worker in Tamil Nadu for an NGO. We rescue homeless people with mental illness and get them the necessary psychosocial as well as medical treatment they need. If we were able to find their family, then they would be reintegrated with their family or, through other options, reintegrated back into the community.

We often do outreach services in different places to identify homeless people with mental illness, and we receive calls from the community if they spot someone with the specified issues. Then we will go to the place and try to interact with the person in order to help and rescue him or her. If we are not able to rescue the person on the first day, then we will come back regularly and build a rapport with him or her, and we will give him or her time to do the same with us. Once he or she is willing to accompany us, we will take him or her to the rehabilitation centre after the initial medical check-up from the medical college.

One day in 2021, we got a call from one of our supporters in the community saying that there was a man around forty to forty-five years old who seemed to have a mental illness. We reached the place, met the person, and tried interacting with him. He was very calm and cooperative. He said his name was Husain. The people around him told us that he was from Kerala, and he had been in that place for almost twenty years. He came there when he was around fourteen to fifteen years old, and they don't know how he got there. He was having tea when we met him. When asked whether he wanted anything more in Tamil, he didn't respond, but when asked in Malayalam, he said he wanted something to eat. So, we bought him some tea and asked him whether he would come with us to our centre, and he said he would. We rescued him and took him to the Medical College for his initial physical check-up and routine blood work; usually, people who get rescued are mostly restless during these check-ups because of being with so many people and being their centre of attraction. But Husain was cooperative throughout the procedure. Later, Husain was admitted to our centre.

Initially, Husain didn't talk much. We were able to rebuild his self-care routine, and he also helped others at the centre. He used to hoard things like sticks or torn clothes in his cupboard and made doll-like things with them. He was responding to the medication positively, and we were able to observe great improvements in his overall behaviour. In the first month, we tried to get information about him and his family from Husain, but we were not successful. But Husain started to interact with us and others in the facility more and got involved in different activities, too.

When it comes to getting details about a person's life before they become homeless, it is a very difficult process, as most of the people have been away from home and without proper treatment for so many years. There are people who have been away from home for five or ten years, and sometimes more than that. Being homeless for such a long time with no proper treatment for their mental illness will end up with most of them forgetting about their family and the details of where their home is. As a result, finding out details about them and their family becomes a tiring task. And sometimes, no matter how much effort we put in or how many people we reach out to, it will not yield the desired result, and subsequently, we will have to look into other long-term options for their reintegration into the community. The interesting thing about collecting these details is that there is no guarantee that you will get an answer. For example, if you ask them where their home is, some people will say that it's India, just say a state's name, or sometimes tell the name of the place where their home is, not the district or state, and oftentimes these places may not be well known, and even if we try to Google them, there won't be any results. No matter how many times you ask the same question or ask for the district, you get the same answer. So, then you have to modify the question; instead of asking where their home is, we ask if we take a bus or an auto, where we should get off, etc. And even if we don't get the result on the first try, in many cases, there will be positive outcomes.

In Husain's case, it was not different than usual. We were unable to obtain his personal or family details other than his name for the first two months. Husain was very sociable with others, but he was not very talkative. This was also making it difficult for us to get more details from him. But gradually, through medication, counselling, and different activities, he started to trust us, and he realized that we were only trying to help him find his family and get him back home safely. He started mentioning a quite famous place in Kerala, and when asked further, 'If we take an auto from this place, then exactly where should we get down?' he gave the name of the place, which was exactly where his home was. He gave the names of his father, mother, and brothers. Then we contacted the police station in that place and passed on the information given by Husain along with his photo. Then we waited for them to call back with a positive response. We didn't have to wait very long; they called us back by the end of the day and informed us that they had found Husain's family and gave us his brother's number. We immediately called the number, and also, as per the family's request, we did a video call too. Husain's family was so happy to see him, and he also identified his family.

From his brother, we got the details about how Husain ended up in Tamil Nadu. Husain started having mental health issues in his early twenties. The family did seek medical treatment, and while he was in the hospital, he would take the medicine and be fine to go home, but after returning home, he would stop taking the medicine and become aggressive. His wife also left him because of his mental illness. Husain once threw a stone at a bus, shattering the front glass. After this incident, the natives instructed Husain's family to take him to Ervadi, a place in Tamil Nadu known for faith healing for people with mental illness. This incident happened in 2002. As instructed by the people, Husain was taken to Ervadi by his father and brother. When they reached Ervadi, they learned that the place was closed because of a tragic fire accident that happened there in 2001, which led to the deaths of twenty-eight people with mental illness. Husain's family was informed that there were no new admissions to the place, and therefore they couldn't help them.

Husain's family was disappointed, and they returned to the hotel that they were staying in. In the evening, they went to a nearby tea shop to have tea. The owner of the tea shop noticed that they were from Kerala, and he inquired about the purpose of their visit to Ervadi. Husain's family told him about his mental illness and the issues that happened in their native country. After hearing all these, the shop owner noticed that Husain was very calm, and he suggested that Husain should stay and work in his shop. The family was fine with this decision, and Husain also didn't have any issues with it. That being so, the family decided to regularly visit Husain in the tea shop in Ervadi. They left Husain in the shop owner's care and came back to Kerala. They regularly visited Husain, and he was doing fine and working well in the tea shop. But all this changed on December 26, 2004.

On December 26, 2004, at 7:59 a.m. local time, an undersea earthquake with a magnitude of 9.1 struck off the coast of the Indonesian island of Sumatra. Over the next seven hours, a tsunami, a series of immense ocean waves triggered by the earthquake, reached out across the Indian Ocean, devastating coastal areas as far away as East Africa. Some locations reported that the waves had reached a height of thirty feet (nine metres) or more when they hit the shoreline. The number of deaths reported in India alone was 2,27,898. The states affected were Kerala, Tamil Nadu, Andhra Pradesh, Pondicherry, and the Andaman and Nicobar Islands.

Ervadi was also one of the places affected by the tsunami. Many people died and lost their homes, and a lot of people also went missing, and the authorities were not able to find them or their dead bodies. Husain was one of those missing people. His family went to Ervadi in search of him but never found him or his remains. There have been incidents of people who got misplaced due to the tsunami returning after a while, and Husain's family also believed that he may return soon. But even after five years, there was no information about Husain, and they had to believe that he must have perished in the 2004 tsunami.

After a long sixteen years, they received a call from the police station saying that someone had found Husain and that he was still in Tamil Nadu. His family couldn't believe the news because there had been no news about Husain and his whereabouts for more than a decade, and suddenly they received information that he was alive, which was almost a miracle for them. They didn't believe Husain was alive until they video-called us and saw him. Husain was also happy to finally see his family and talked to them. His brother and cousin immediately decided to come and take Husain back home. They arrived within three to four days and were so happy to see Husain. They talked to the social workers and the doctors regarding his treatment and were delighted to know that Husain was well taken care of and was also undergoing treatment for his mental illness. The doctor explained in detail Husain's problem, the treatment given to him, and the instructions for further treatment, including medicines for one month. After saying goodbye to others in the centre, Husain was going back to his home and family and his life after sixteen years of abandonment and suffering.

Husain was lucky enough to have a happy ending and finally went back to his family. But this is not always the case. There have been people who were not able to go home with their families, not for lack of trying; even after exhausting all the resources we had, we couldn't help them. But as mentioned earlier, we would find alternative rehabilitation options for them. In the beginning, I said that small actions can make a significant difference, and this story has been a perfect example. When we went to rescue Husain, the people in that community who had been taking care of him by providing him food, clothes, and shelter, as well as grooming him occasionally, were very protective of him. Without knowing all the details about us and the centre, they were not willing to send Husain with us. They didn't have to be concerned about a homeless person and could have ignored him like many do, but their little acts of kindness helped him survive for more than a decade. The person who informed us about Husain or the tea shop owner—his small actions have made such a huge difference in Husain's life.

Every time we rescue someone from the street and bring him or her to the centre, we have the hope that we will be able to find his or her family and reunite them. This won't happen all the time, but no matter what, we still have hope, and hope can make such a huge impact. Many live in the hope of a better tomorrow, and often hope is the thing that inspires people to move forward.

*****

Author's Message

These lines by Emily Dickinson are very close to my heart, and I would suggest them to my dear readers.

"Hope is the thing with feathers,

that perches in the soul,

and sings the tune without the words,

and never stops at all".

[P.N: - Character's name changed for confidentiality.]

ARTICLES

17

FREEDOM TO CHOOSE

Uma Iyer

Parenthood is a life-changing event that turns our lives completely around. It is a journey that requires huge sacrifices and, in turn, gives happy, fulfilling returns. A journey full of joy, bittersweet moments, tears, laughter, and being forced to grow up, grow old, and experience everything in between. It is a journey that takes us back to our childhood days but with the attitude and points of view of our parents. Because as we grow older, we realize that we are experiencing with our children what our parents experienced with us as children: a journey that is like a rebirth, a life reborn, for a new life to be born from us. And it is a *lifelong* journey.

But what happens when one does not want to embark on this journey? A journey is a journey, and not everyone wants to travel through all the phases of life. Does that become wrong or unjustified? Is it against society and culture? Does everyone need to feel the desire to have a child? Maybe not!

One of my cousins and her husband have decided not to have children at all. This bold decision of theirs is not going down within the family. It is quite understandable since parents always want their kids to get married and have children of their own. I happened to ask her about this decision of theirs, and she simply said, *'Both I and my husband do not have the patience, tolerance, and natural parental instincts that are required to take care of a baby. Just because the family wants us to have kids, we cannot go ahead and ruin a child's life and everyone else's after bringing it into this world. We don't think we can give the kind of love and care children always need. We are not sorry about this decision. It is our decision.'*

'Is it because of your job, your career goals, or something like that?' I asked because these are the reasons that we feel are a hindrance in decision-making. But my cousin was confident and clear. *'No! Not at all! It is not at all for our job, career, or lack of time; it is simply that we do not feel like having one.'*

I could agree with her. After all, it is her life and their lives. What they want to do with it is their decision. But I must salute her boldness and courage. She knows she will be talked about. People who do not know about their decision will think she or her husband probably has fertility issues. They will receive tonnes and tonnes of unsolicited advice, opinions, doctor recommendations, and suggestions to visit spiritual and religious centres that can give them a kid if they pay a visit and everything under the sun, just so that they can have a child. But! But she is not concerned about anything.

A practical decision.

And then there is this friend who has taken the decision not to go to any lengths to have a child. She is firm about not letting her body go through the pain of IVF or similar processes. She and her husband are aware that without medical intervention, the chances of them becoming parents are next to nil. But they are sure of the fact that at no cost will they allow her to go through so much pain, both physically and emotionally. They have left it to nature to work a miracle. And if nature doesn't help, they have decided that they will adopt a child. But they do not have the support of their families for adoption. They are stuck with the idea until the families get convinced. But for the sake of becoming biological parents, they will not go through this.

A practical and emotional decision.

And then I have my cousin, who has been unable to have kids even after more than fifteen years of marriage. The couple knows by now quite clearly that it is not possible for them to have kids. After numerous rounds of medical intervention and failures, they have given up trying. But they are also clear about not wanting to adopt a child. They feel they will not be able to love the adopted child as much as their own. A biological child is a biological child, and just to have a child to call their own, they will not adopt. Being childless is preferable to them than adopting.

If I come to think of it, does having children really define us as human beings? Married or unmarried, we all have our own place and identity in this world. So, why is there this compulsion to have kids?

In today's time, people take their time getting married and settling down in their lives. The need for personal growth and personal space has become dominant. It is a time when people prefer to be single mothers and single fathers by adopting children without wanting the baggage of marriage. So, if a married couple decides against having a child, it is a practical and logical decision that they must have taken using their own brains and feelings. If they don't have the time, let them be. If they don't have the inclination, let them be. If they are career-oriented and ambitious and have other goals in life, let them pursue those. They are doing what seems wise to them. Let us not define their lives with our definitions. It's their dictionary of life, with their own meanings.

For me, these examples are freedom in the real sense. Despite the fact that everyone starts asking about children just after a few months of marriage and continues with the inquiries even years after marriage, these couples have made a stand and are happy and satisfied with their decisions. The satisfaction, confidence, and happiness they live with is real freedom.

*****

Author's Message

The freedom to choose to have or not to have a child must be left to the married couples.

18

THE (LOST) MOTHER IN MOTHERHOOD

V. Rashmi Rao

Motherhood is a wonderful phase in a woman's life, but at the same time, it brings with it several challenges. It is said that "when a baby is born, a mother is born too". This fact is absolutely true. Just as the baby is new to this world, the mother is also new to the experience she is going through.

The birth of a baby brings mountains of happiness, excitement, and bliss, but it also brings curiosity, insecurity, anxiety, and irritability issues for mothers. Mothers often bear the burden of caring for the infant while also struggling with how to care for themselves.

When we speak about mental illness, we usually discuss depression, anxiety, sadness, loneliness, headaches, and heartbreaks, but we never discuss the pain a new-born mother goes through. Even the doctor who assists in her birth and cares for her for the entire nine months frequently forgets or fails to mention postpartum depression (PPD); a serious mental illness that mothers face soon after childbirth.

'Why am I even focusing on this?' you must be thinking. Our mothers, aunts, or generations before us never experienced PPD or postpartum mental trauma, so why would we? The times are changing, families are becoming smaller, stress levels are increasing, and so are illnesses.

Before we understand PPD, let us first know some quick facts about depression. Usually, casually and socially, "mental illness" or "depression" is muddled with "emotional stability" and "psychological health", but it isn't all the same. Mental illness occurs when there are certain biological changes inside the brain that cause a person to behave or act differently. This may include depression, impaired functioning, and other alterations in behaviour.

Why are you and me or anyone depressed? Or why do we feel low, sad, and lonely?

It is normal for a person to feel sad, lonely, and disinterested in daily activities, and these feelings can be confused with depression symptoms. You may feel there is a full stop to your life. Soon your self-esteem starts dropping, and you start losing confidence in the little things you do.

Age has nothing to do with depression. Anyone, at any age, in any phase of life can experience it. Children as young as five years old can suffer from depression. Although it's just a phase for some and can go after a while, for many it can stay for a longer period, and they need therapy and medication to come out of it. The symptoms and reasons for being depressed are different for men, women, children, teenagers, and old adults, which means the treatment and recovery time would be different for everyone.

What is Postpartum Depression (PPD)?

For me, it was really hard to figure out that I was suffering from PPD. Yes, you read it right; I went through the hard phase of PPD.

A woman's body undergoes numerous changes during and after pregnancy. Childbirth isn't easy for her. She is constantly fighting to take care of herself and the baby at the same time. After childbirth, mothers experience PPD for three to five days; this is also called "Baby Blues". PPD is a common experience for mothers, but if the mother continues to feel the same way, such as being lonely, often sad, empty, and unable to love her new child, it's time to see a therapist. In my case, I couldn't personally visit a therapist as it was the COVID-19 phase, so I dealt with it all by myself.

PPD is a serious mental condition, and some mothers even get anxiety disorders. Research suggests that one in every nine new mothers suffers from PPD. Mothers can feel disconnected from their babies, and it can also affect their day-to-day activities.

Let me share some stereotypes related to PPD that I personally experienced:

1. PPD is only in the first few days after childbirth

This statement isn't completely false. For some, PPD lasts a few days and then disappears, but for others, it lasts much longer than expected. I didn't realize I had PPD at first, but as the days passed, I realized I was falling apart, crying more often, getting irritated over trivial matters, being disturbed, shouting, and becoming angry frequently. I used to get thoughts of hurting my child and myself. I had sleep deprivation, had no energy, and always felt too tired and less motivated. I withdrew from myself, my friends, and my family, and I always felt guilty for behaving like this. I knew that this wasn't correct, and I had to do something to get out of it. Thanks to my husband, my mother, and my loved ones who listened to me and understood I was "not okay". They helped me overcome the situation in the best possible way, and today I'm able to share my journey here.

2. PPD will fade away on its own over time

I myself have been a victim of PPD. I've had a lot of difficulties dealing with my mental illness while also caring for my child. Dealing with my PPD was the biggest challenge for me, as I had to look after my daughter, myself, and my family. Losing myself to some depression meant putting my entire family at risk. So, what did I do to overcome this PPD? It wasn't easy, and neither is it easy to fight with yourself, go against your own mind and win over your challenges, but it isn't impossible either. If I can, you can too!

I worked hard and continue to work on myself on a daily basis to be mentally fit rather than physically fit. To be at peace with myself; to be able to calm my body, mind, and soul; to be able to understand things and situations in a more composed manner; to be able to become a better ME every day.

3. PPD means I stop loving my child and will harm him or her

This is actually a myth. Mothers suffering from PPD do feel that they may not be able to love their children or that they are not caring enough, which I felt too. Sometimes I used to get scared, thinking that my actions might harm my child, which was completely wrong. But experts say there isn't any connection between PPD and a mother's love for her child. Often, postpartum psychosis is confused with PPD, where a mother loses touch with her real life and may harm her babies. This is a rare condition, though. However, because of PPD, the bond between me and my daughter was deteriorating.

In this article, I have shared a few tips that worked for me to overcome PPD and become a better version of myself:

1. Get educated: Before you plan to become a mother and during the pregnancy phase, read, learn, and understand all the phases of pregnancy. The pros. and cons. Most doctors, even the best ones, fail to educate new mothers about PPD. They tell you what to eat and what not to eat, and how to care for the baby, but no one talks about PPD. Mothers-in-law at home ignore this because they haven't experienced it or have

incorrect information about it. Talk to your doctor, midwife, or read about it.

2. Look for signs of postpartum: A mother's first responsibility is her child, but she also needs to focus on herself. If you feel or experience any of the symptoms, seek help immediately. Get help from anyone and everyone; tell them you are not okay, and you need support. Tell your husband, mother, mother-in-law, or whoever is nearby, how you are feeling.

3. Practice meditation: As we practice prenatal yoga, postpartum yoga, and meditation, it is also a must that we practice both. This will help you keep your mind, body, and soul at peace. Everyone knows the benefits of yoga and meditation, so practice them regularly. This helped me a lot.

4. Recreate a childhood pastime: In the entire postpartum phase till now, there have been good days, bad days, sad days, and happy days. Your child's demands are different every day, and you may not get them at the same time. So, whenever I get time, I paint and create something from scratch that I put my mind and heart into. My complete concentration is on designing that piece. Learn music and practice dancing.

5. Read and write: When you want to keep yourself busy, the best things to do are to read and write. Read good, positive, and motivational books that will help you calm your mind. Whereas writing helps you put your thoughts into words. Being a writer, I write often. Writing makes me happy and helps me to channel my thought process.

6. Exercise: We are all aware of the benefits of exercising, so why not make it a ritual? Go for a morning or evening walk in a nearby park; you can take your baby along. Join a gym if possible or do some yoga. Any kind of exercise will help you relax your stressed muscles.

7. Join a club: These days, many cities have "Mommy Clubs",

where they invite new mothers with or without their children. They organize fun games, educate mothers in several areas, and give mothers a platform to speak up.

8. Being judged: Many people will judge you for several reasons; let them. You have become a new mother; your body will change, your thought process will be different, and so will your behaviour. For you, your baby matters. So, ignore the crowd and move ahead.

Lastly, understand that motherhood isn't easy, and no one ever said that it would be simple. You know yourself the best, and you also know what's best for the baby. So, if things aren't going as planned and you're feeling down and depressed, just slow down; no one and nothing is perfect. Start analysing the situation and slowly work on it. You will get through!

*****

Author's Message

Our babies need us more than anyone else in this world. They will be this small for only a few more years, and this shall pass. Happy motherhood and happy parenting!

19

THE UNHEARD VOICE: WOMEN

V. Rashmi Rao

In the land of goddesses like Lakshmi and Saraswati, with freedom fighters like Begum Hazrat Mahal, Jhansi ki Rani, and Ahilya Bai Holkar, women are still being left behind, unheard, unwanted, misunderstood, and disliked. They are still fighting daily to be the best, to be capable enough, to prove themselves, and to make people around them understand how important they are and how difficult it is for them to keep themselves going.

My article is about a common woman found in every household, rich or poor. She is a daughter, a sister, a wife, a mother, and most importantly, the "driver" of the house. Yes, I'm denoting a woman as a driver because, in a more real and practical sense, a woman is the only person who drives the house in all directions, shifting the gears at the correct time, and breaking wherever necessary.

Housewife, homemaker, stay-at-home mother—whatever you name her, she is the one who builds the house from scratch, brick by brick. As long as a woman has the capacity to bear children, society believes her primary responsibility is to give birth to a child and take care of the house. If she does these two things, it is considered a feat for a woman.

India has been celebrating its independence from British rule for seventy-six years, but are Indian women truly free? Are they independent enough to take their own decisions, live life on their terms, and be free as a bird, not under any kind of pressure, power, or emotional attachment?

There have been several books written, articles published, and movies made about women and their sufferings. Gender inequality has always been a hot topic of discussion, but when it comes to implementation, very few would actually value women for who they are. We have a long, in-depth history in our country associated with women and the sacrifices they have made to prove and create a space for themselves. But somewhere, we are still failing to give women the basic rights they deserve.

I don't mean to go into detail about the equal number of seats they should have on local buses, reservations for job roles, or other perks, but rather their very existence in society. The Hindu Code Bill has approved the right to an equal share of parental property for both the daughter and the son. The Marriage Act articulates that women can no longer be viewed as the property of men. Marriage is now being considered a personal concern, and if any one of the partners feels discontented, she or he has the right to get separated and file for divorce. Law is relatively simple to pass when compared to how it is absorbed by everyone in a society where herd mentality and collective thinking are prevalent. To prove themselves equal to men in society and to enjoy the same rights with the utmost dignity and standing, the laws in the Indian Constitution must be changed, and in order to achieve this change, they must break free from the bonds of slavery and superstitions.

A civilization can be best judged by the way it treats the women in its society. Similarly, a house is judged by the way a woman is treated inside it.

Let's meet four different women who are trying to lead a basic, normal life.

Jayanti is an average-looking girl from a wealthy family with many members. She was brought up in an environment where girls have to follow whatever the males in the family say. Although she was lucky enough to be allowed to go to school, college, and even work in a male-dominated society, she still has no personal choices or opinions. She struggles daily to be independent, to be happy, to be herself, and to be who she actually wants to be. She tries to find answers to all the unheard questions, but the only choice she is left with is to listen to her family. Why can't Jayanti take her own decisions, live life on her terms, and be free enough to be happy?

Another woman, Ronita, grew up in an upper-middle-class family with a brother and a mother. She lost her father pretty early in her life. She fought all odds—the daily hardships of getting a job, staying in the job, earning money, getting married, and trusting men. It wasn't easy for Ronita to trust men, as she just knew the only man in her life was her father, to whom she confided all her secrets and whom she loved more than anyone else in this world. His loss created a void in her life that couldn't be filled by some random guy. After some failures, she trusted a man and got married too. Now this man is good at character, humble in behaviour, and wealthy enough to take good care of the family, but he is a "Man". Ronita is happy with a wonderful husband and a kid, but still, she feels lost and lonely all the time as her life revolves around these two humans. There is a full stop to her personal life, her career, her ambition, and her interests. Being a wife and a mother, she is stuck inside the house doing the same mundane activities. Although her husband is a good man, he is unable to understand the situation Ronita is going through or the daily fight she is having with herself. This does not mean he does not care at all, but he does not realize the emotional roller coaster his wife is going through. Why can't Ronita's husband understand her problem? Why can't he support her in her career by sharing her tasks and taking care of the child? Is Ronita expecting and asking for too much?

Shanaya is a well-educated married middle-aged woman. She has two lovely children who live with her in a developed country (Korea).

Her well-off husband handles everything around the house. Shanaya has a huge friend circle and a decent social life. With a master's degree in business and research, Shanaya always feels she is meant to do different things in her career, but instead, she is sitting at home doing nothing but cooking, cleaning, and taking care of the family. She isn't allowed to speak with random people or even her maternal family back in her own country. Why? There isn't a specific reason, just a male ego, as Shanaya's family failed to meet her husband's expectations. He thinks that just because he is the man of the house, he always needs special treatment and all the luxuries around him. After serving them for fifteen years, Shanaya now has "permission" to step outside and work for herself. Why did she have to wait for fifteen long years, and why does she need permission to work?

Pareenita is a straightforward, extremely talented girl. She is married into a modern family where education and a professional career are top priorities. She has the freedom to do everything but has no right to decide whether she should have a child or focus on her career and personal goals. Being a woman, she is asked to step down, take a setback in her career, have a child, and focus on family life. Is she happy being like this? The answer may be no, but she still survives to live with the same husband and family.

When we read through these four stories, we may relate to the situation and the pain these four women are going through. The most common trait is that they are all fighting for survival. Bookish education isn't enough for men in our country; we need to teach them and make them understand that women inside or outside the house need respect, space, appreciation, applause, freedom, motivation, and support—to be heard, to be able to speak and to be able to live.

Courage only comes when you have the right support at the right time from the right people, and you know you can rely on them at any time. When a female child is born, she requires the support of her father and brother to feel safe, understood, and confident that she can do whatever she wants. When she marries, she expects her husband to help her with daily tasks, understand her, and assist her in making decisions between her personal and professional lives.

Women can reveal their hidden courage and strength all the more when they are self-centred, focused, and supported by the men around them. I know we are talking about being independent here, but somewhere we all have to seek help. They must tear open the cocoon to get out and breathe in the fresh air outside.

A single spark can start a big fire, and likewise, a single woman can bring about the change she wants. The revolution starts with her being strong and decisive. These four women will mature in their respective lives and survive the battles they are currently facing. Jayanti will create her own happy world as soon as she believes in herself and is free to make her own decisions. Ronita hopes her husband will understand the pain she is going through and will support her more, but her expectations will only be met when she works on herself and focuses on her priorities. Although Shanaya got permission to work after all her struggles, she still needs to compromise on a few things. Pareenita is handling her situations beautifully, and with all the conventions around her, she is still turning her life into a wonderful story. Hope is still alive in these women that they will make their lives better. They are all happy in their current lives, but with a little push, they will make themselves happier.

I believe a woman has been a warrior since birth, from Sita to Lakshmi Bai to modern-day women. They have evolved to be better warriors and have opted for several methods to fulfil their dreams. Let us help each other so that we can help a woman somewhere.

✶✶✶✶✶

Author's Message

"Yatra naryastu pujyante raman tetatra devata"
("Where women are honoured, there the deities are pleased.")

20

OH, IT'S PERIOD!

V. Rashmi Rao

A period has different meanings in various subjects a human has ever come across. But for women, "period" is a sin, a taboo, a punishment, and a monthly occurring process. Women and men both don't speak and utter the word "period". It's like they have given it many names, like "chumps", and if they are in public, they say "shh" or "don't say it loudly".

Period, menstruation, or the menstrual cycle is a biological and natural process that all women experience. There are some of them who need to deal with the "period" and its related problems for nearly ten days a month while still being expected to remain silent, clean, and part of the religious, cultural, and so-called "pure" society.

Research over the years has shown that not all women get periods, and there are some transgender people who also experience periods. You'd be surprised to learn that many people, including our family members or the men in our family, are unaware of periods or menstruation in general. They just know that something happens to us (women) every month and we are restricted from doing things like going to the kitchen, going to the holy places, worshipping, not touching things, getting close to our partner, etc. etc., and the list goes on.

Women, especially in India, have been following superstitions, rituals, and practices relating to menstruation for ages. Many people, including myself, our mothers, and other women in the house, are unsure why we perform these rituals in particular. Many women have tried asking questions about these menstrual rituals but have been defined and ignored as modern and unworthy women to move around in society.

As per research menstruation is a bodily function that has helped a woman restrict her mobility during those days, helping her to take care of herself. There is also a mention of this in the holy books of Hindus. Moreover, in various Indian cultures, menstruation was considered an auspicious thing, and even today, there are several communities in India that celebrate this occasion when a girl menstruates for the first time. Somewhere through the years, the same humans and communities that celebrate and worship women started restricting and punishing them for their miraculous bodies and ability to create mere human existence.

How did women start bleeding on a monthly basis? The origin

Our Indian mythology explains menstruation and connects it to a story that dates back to Vedic times. In a small fight, a sage named Vritas was killed at the hands of Indradev. This meant Indradev committed the crime of killing a Brahmin, or "brahma-hatya". To get out of the sin, he worshipped Lord Vishnu, and his prayers were answered. Lord Vishnu advised him to split the load of his crime into earth, trees, water, and women.

As stated in a popular Sanskrit text, "The Vashistha Dharmasutra", there was a water demon incident that dominates a woman's place in today's society. It states, "A woman is not independent; she is a slave to the men who are her masters".

Women are restricted during their menstruation cycle because it is believed that they are polluted and impure during these four to five days. They treat a bleeding woman as a bad thing, and they think that if a woman these days touches or sees anything, it will make them polluted or impure.

Women are still suffering as a result of the consequences of this ancestral philosophy that has been passed down through generations. We as women are so embarrassed, afraid, and want to hide anything related to periods that we rarely discuss it openly. To date, sanitary pads or tampons are covered in plastic wrap or paper. What are we really hiding here—the most necessary hygienic product or the fact that women bleed monthly for five days, which is a natural biological phenomenon?

The science behind menstruation

Did you know? Menstruation is not associated with gender! It's a natural biological process that occurs in humans having a reproductive system, and this largely happens in women, so it's a women's issue. It is well known that in transgender people, menstruation induces feelings of dysphoria, and to avoid or hide this, many transgender people undergo several hormonal therapies. There are reasons like financial hardship, lack of education, and personal choice that affect the decision to accept these hormonal therapies to stop periods in transgender people. But not all of them opt for it, and neither of these therapies guarantees to stop periods. This means there are men across the globe who bleed. Yes, you heard it right—men bleed too!

A celebration that comes with pain

Menarche, as it is defined in the dictionary, is the first time a girl menstruates. This is regarded as a milestone in a woman's life since her birth. This also means that a girl has grown up and moved into womanhood.

Previously, the first menstruation was celebrated to inform people and society that their girl has matured and is now of "marriageable age", with her parents looking for potential partners.

As a female from the southern part of the country, I understand how grand this event is. In Telangana and Andhra Pradesh, it is called "Peddamanishi Pandaga", "Half-Saree Function", or "Odhni Function". The function is celebrated usually on the first day, the fifth day, and the last day if the bleeding goes on for seven or ten days of the menstrual cycle. It starts with a "mangal snan", or bath, given by five women that excludes her mother. While all this process is going on, the girl has to stay inside a separate room as she is bleeding, and she is forbidden from touching or roaming around in other areas of the house, especially the puja room and kitchen. During these 5 days, she has to sleep on a different mattress, use separate vessels, and eat on a separate plate. On the last day, the girl is showered with gifts like a saree, jewellery, and other necessities.

It is hard to believe and surprising to learn that there are more than forty different restrictions that include touch, food, and women's participation and mobility in society and inside the home. Due to such restrictions, several women have lost their lives. Women across India have been suffering from nutritional deficits, reproductive issues, mental health concerns, and a lack of educational and occupational opportunities. They have lost their dignity and mental peace under the burden and name of tradition or ritual and have lived with chronic humiliation and inferiority complexes their entire lives.

Breaking age-old cultural taboos and rituals was, is, and will never be easy. In India, questioning a ritual, a religious belief, or a family practice is itself a big taboo. How dare you raise a question against your elders! We've been listening to it since we were born. Going against a ritual is going against culture and society. However, these cultures entirely fail to convince me and other women as to why we are excluded, prohibited, and stigmatized.

What can we do?

Several Hindu communities in India claim that if women on their periods touch pickles, sweets, or certain foods while menstruating, the food will spoil; pickles may turn sour; women are not allowed to eat curd, tamarind, or pickles as they may affect the blood flow; not permitted to touch drinking water. It is also believed that a woman's body releases some rays and smells that may contaminate the food. Breaking this myth is important. Women should be given fresh and healthy foods during these days so that their bodies get some energy to fight the pains and problems associated with periods. Softer foods rich in iron and calcium should be consumed more.

There are gurus and saints who say the actual reason women are not allowed to visit temples is that women are themselves goddesses, and when they visit temples during their periods, the energy present in the stone idol gets transferred to the women, and thus the idol becomes lifeless with zero energy, and there is no point left in the mere existence of the temple. It has nothing to do with blood impurity, bad omens, or evil spirits. When I first got my periods after my marriage, my mother-in-law covered the idols of God with cloth, as she believed that if my shadow fell on them, they would become impure, and I would get a curse for doing so. But we must believe that "God is one, and worship is for everyone". Devipuram is a temple in Andhra Pradesh founded by Sri Amritananda Natha Saraswati (Guruji), who says that Devipuram is dedicated to Devi, where most of the priests are women, and they are free to worship and visit the temple whenever they want. The Kamakhya temple in Guwahati is built in the shape of a woman's vagina, and it is said that the Devi bleeds every four days. People, whether or not they get periods, irrespective of gender, visit this temple.

More space, time, and comfort should be given so that women can speak and discuss more about periods and their related concerns. Starting with mothers and females at home, the teachers in school, caregivers, doctors, friends, family, and colleagues in the office, women shouldn't be afraid of speaking about their periods to anyone. Making women know how necessary it is to be hygienic during these days and how they can be clean and healthy is important.

We must understand that the real reason for periods is the ovulation process, which is triggered by a missed chance of pregnancy and further results in blood flow from the endometrial vessels, followed by the preparation of the reproductive organ for the next cycle. Thus, there is no such proof or reason for menstruating women to be called or considered "impure", and there is no need for purification. Educating women about menstruation is more important than purifying them.

*****

Author's Message

There isn't any proof or specific explanation, if all this is true, of women being impure, contaminating food, or getting cursed by gods. Understanding them, their emotional and hormonal changes, educating them, taking care of them, and respecting them must be a definite reality.

21

DOMESTIC VIOLENCE: WHY IT IS PORTRAYED AS NORMAL?

Kirti S Wadhwa

Domestic violence is not a societal or political issue. It is a question of a woman's individuality, the suppressed voices of girls or women who have experienced it, voices that remain suppressed within the four walls of their so-called home, voices that are never heard. Domestic violence is more than just the marks on a woman's body. The silent abuse has a significant psychological and emotional impact on them. They battle with their own fears—fear of touch, abuse, and noise. The scars we can only see and the pain we can never feel.

According to the Crime in India Report, in 2021, the crime rate against women in India was 64.5%[1]. NFHS-5 data says that 45% of Indian women and 44% of Indian men justify the husband beating his wife[2]. This is more than just a statistic; it is an indication that, while things are changing—women are now more educated and employed—and strict laws have been enacted, the situation is direly in need of improvement.

When education is used to better society and equity is believed and practised, it is advantageous. The intersectionality of gender bias,

---

[1] National Crime Records Bureau. (2021). *Crime in India* 2021. Ministry of Home Affairs.

[2] Ministry of Health and Family Welfare. (2021). *National Family Health Survey* (NFHS-5) 2019-21. Government of India.

cultural practices, and the socio-economic status of women in society degrades their quality of life.

Domestic violence does not only affect the present generation but also becomes a vicious cycle of assault in the family and community, leading to its normalization. Even today, in some parts of the world, including India, there exists a population with rudimentary thinking, entangled with a bunch of pathetic rituals, and a society where women's tolerance of violence is adulated.

Let's delve into this concept through a fictional story.

This story is about the Osmanabad district in Maharashtra, famous for its rituals, festivals, customs, and cultural beliefs. Over the years, the district had become a hub for tourism and research on its cultural practices and their association with literacy rates, health outcomes, and financial outcomes. Due to its gradual increase in popularity, the district was able to generate economic opportunities.

Ironically, there were few villages in this district where the cultural practices were against the law and women were treated as slaves. During the celebrations, the only sounds heard were those of drunken men shouting and abusing each other. Nobody had ever focused on these areas of the district.

One day, a group of researchers and social workers took on the job of discovering female-related practices for a project, trying to find out why the literacy rate was so low. Upon arrival, they spoke with the local authority about the region, the customs, the villages, and the distinctive characteristics of each hamlet. They painted a flowery picture of the village. So, the researchers went one step ahead and tried mingling with locals, especially women. Females in the village seem hesitant to converse. This increased their curiosity, so they decided to live in one of the villages for a few days. The local authority warned them as the group had female members. A post office clerk said, 'Sir Ji, you have women team members; you don't know the men of the village.' I would suggest, 'Don't go.'

But the team had a job to do, so they decided to plan a field visit to the location. There was uncomfortable negativity in the air. The village had a primary school but no teachers. The building's state, with broken windowpanes, spoke for itself.

They reached me on a Sunday evening, around 6 p.m. It was dark and silent. People were staring at them strangely. The next day, they saw something unexpected. Every woman in the village had marks on her body. The majority of the adolescent girls were either pregnant or already had children. These girls looked too undernourished to carry or nurse the baby. Some had scars on their faces or hands, and some had been burned. The majority of the males, both young and old, were involved in alcohol or drug addiction. This was something the team was not ready for.

They found it difficult to communicate with the people over there. After staying for three days, the female members started experiencing verbal abuse that initially they tried to ignore, but the situation worsened when they were threatened by the young boys, supported by the adult males. The main reason was that these girls were trying to form a bond with the women in the village, understand their issues, and support them. Village women were still silent, for they were aware of the repercussions of opening their mouths. Only a very few of the women shared their experiences hesitantly when alone. Here is a snapshot of two such stories:

Story 1: Sana and her ruined childhood.

Sana is fourteen years old. She has one younger brother, who is twelve. Sana was beaten up with a belt and shoes by her brother. Her father was an alcoholic who frequently physically abused Sana and her mother. Sana's mother, Shalu, never raised her voice, neither for herself nor for her daughter. At fifteen, Sana was made to marry a man just double her age. Sana, seventeen, is the mother of a one-year-old daughter and is pregnant with her second child. She is undernourished. She has never received a professional health check-up. The marks on her face depict what she has gone through at such a young age. Her daughter's future is as bleak as her own.

Story 2: Dowry is not what I just paid for the marriage; it was the beginning of something more—the story of Jaya.

Jaya was married to Suresh. Thinking that her life would change, she moved in with a new family. Yes, her life changed drastically. Her parents wanted to get rid of her since she was dark-skinned. Why would anyone marry a brown girl without material benefits? Her parents had taken out a loan to pay for her dowry. This enhanced the confidence of Jaya's in-laws, and henceforth their materialistic demands skyrocketed. As a result, her parents severed all ties with her. Her husband, furious because he thought Jaya was his cash cow, started beating her. One day, when she raised her voice, Suresh burned her left arm. Jaya was unable to get pregnant, which made her situation even more awful. Later, the family decided to lock her in a room, claiming she was mentally sick, and remarry Suresh. This story was told by Meena, a resident of the same village. Jaya was living in abysmal ignorance, locked in her room with the bare minimum of food, and one day she committed suicide.

There must be many such harrowing stories in this village. The researchers were unable to dive further after listening to them. Also, the verbal abuse towards the female researchers escalated to physical assault, including stone-throwing and threats of death. Within a week, the team decided to return to their city since they were terrified and worried. Female researchers were especially traumatized. After taking a few days' breaks, they decided to go back to the village and help those women. This time, they would be more attentive and would have to coordinate with different government and non-government bodies. Soon, they mapped out the way and developed their plan of action. They went to the village with proper government orders.

The research team collaborated with an NGO and started an educational and women's empowerment program. The women were initially made aware of their sufferings. They were made aware of their constitutional right to education. The team supported them in engaging in conversations with each other and sharing their experiences. Alongside, they were taught basic life skills such as handicrafts, henna tattoos, stitching, etc.—something that would attract tourists. The entire procedure was carried out in full view of the local police.

It's been more than three years since then, and the programme is successfully running. The programme is continued by the women's self-help groups that were created by the team. The situation in this village has now improved so much that none of the girls are married before the age of eighteen. They have a functioning primary healthcare centre and a new primary school. Women are given a phone number to call if they feel threatened. Sensitization of men in the village is still challenging, but substantial progress has been made.

Now, the district is well known by the name *Humaari Womaniya* ("Our Women") due to the pride these women instil in themselves and their daughters.

Though the story was fictional, it was not very far from reality. It depicted the reality that persists in our society. Giving women centre stage was, is, and will continue to be essential for the overall growth and development of any community or nation. This means that we need to create an unbiased and inclusive environment where the rights of women are equally respected and ensured.

*****

Author's Message

Say no to violence and yes to equal respect and equity towards womanhood.

22

ON THE WRONG SIDE

Akhila Mohan CG

Recently, I had an uncomfortable conversation with a friend, who interrupted me, saying, 'If you had not gone through what you have, then you would have been in a much better state.'

Though I kept quiet at her remark, it left me thinking how different my life would have been if I had married the right person the first time.

Maybe I would have been less traumatized. Maybe I would have been a mother by now. Maybe I would have been more successful professionally. Or maybe I would have been less scarred and broken.

But then I thought, aren't these scars, which we carry hidden in our minds and bodies, the very ones that make us more beautiful and powerful? I sighed deeply, relieved that no matter how much I'd suffered, I'd survived.

It is a story that is almost a decade old. When I was younger and naive, I witnessed most of my friends getting married and settling down. At the insistence and advice of my family, I too got married without knowing if I even wanted to get married. And what followed was a brutal, violent marriage of almost a year that ended with the stillbirth of my child and eventually my divorce.

Honestly, my story is just an ordinary one, like many other women's. Action Aid (an NGO working against poverty and injustice worldwide) mentions that one in four young women (aged fifteen to twenty-four years) who have been in a relationship will have already experienced violence by an intimate partner by the time they are in their mid-twenties[1]. This implies that domestic violence is quite common in our societies. But what makes the entire scenario appalling is that it is widely accepted and normalized despite being criminal offences. Violence against women is socially accepted. Many advocate that it is a man's right as well as his duty to keep his wife within her boundaries. I learned this the hard way when I found all my attempts to explain my decision to divorce my former husband were in vain; society blamed me for my fate.

According to a *Hindustan Times report*[2], the National Family Health Survey (NFHS) found that at least 30%—and possibly even more—of women respondents across fourteen states and union territories justified being beaten by their husbands under certain circumstances. What's surprising is that many of these women who normalized their husbands hitting their wives are victims of violence themselves. Some of my aunts and friends who were stuck in a bad marriage were the ones who advocated the idea of staying in a bad marriage the most. Whenever I tried justifying it as wrong, I often met with remarks like how they also had to suffer something similar, but for the sake of family and children, they adjusted and continued to stay in their abusive relationships. I was often given sermons on how women should be the epitome of sacrifice and tolerance and that ideas of self-respect look good only in books and movies. It is unfortunate that they had to sacrifice their happiness for the sake of their children, either to ensure their financial security or due to a lack of family support. And it is unfortunate that whenever something like this happens, our society further victimizes the victims. This is more

---

[1] Pycroft, H. (2022, November 1). *Violence against women: the statistics around the world. Action Aid.*

[2] *Survey shows 30% women across 14 states, UTs justify men beating their wives.* (2021, November 28). Hindustan Times

common with women who are burdened with the tag of being the homemaker. If things go otherwise, the woman is labelled a failure. And many women succumb to this pressure and continue living in the same abusive marriage despite being unhappy. Also, they think that the known devil is better than the unknown devil waiting for them outside once they are all left alone.

There are numerous reasons why people refrain from even uttering the word "divorce". Patriarchy is one of the many reasons. It runs so deep in our families and cultures that we, even as women, fail to acknowledge how detrimental it can be to our physical and mental health and even societal health. Despite our education, talents, and excellence in the professional sphere, many still believe that a woman's primary job is to get married, maintain the sanctity of her marriage, look after her family, and bear and raise children. No matter how progressive we become as a society, the dominant belief is still that a woman's fate depends on how her marriage works out. If it works out well, then good for her; if it doesn't, she is expected and advised to somehow bear it till the end. And if she defies conventions, then she is the one who has gotten off on the wrong side.

One thing we often fail to acknowledge is that it's not only women who are victims of patriarchy, but men are as well. Many people approached me after my divorce to ask how I was coping and if it was all worth it. Contrary to popular belief *"Mard ko dard nahi hota"*, divorce can be just as bad for men's health as it is for women.

Jennifer Weiner once said, "Nobody ever died of divorce." But, on the contrary, if we look around, we will find many who have died because they didn't opt for a divorce. Do you remember Vismaya, the twenty-two-year-old BAMS student from Kollam, Kerala, who committed suicide due to dowry harassment and violence? Or Thushara, the twenty-seven-year-old woman from Karunagapally, near Kollam, Kerala, who weighed just twenty kilograms at the time of her demise on March 21, 2019 ? As per the various media reports, she died allegedly due to starvation, which was forced upon her by her husband and mother-in-law for dowry-related reasons. If not, then do you remember Ayesha, the twenty-three-year-old woman from Gujarat who ended her life by jumping into the Sabarmati River in Ahmedabad after recording a painful confessional video about her failing marriage and her husband's indifference towards her? If not, consider the numerous news reports of women who couldn't break free from abusive marriages after being harassed for dowry-related reasons and eventually being burned alive. Or think of men who have gone into depression or committed suicide because they were stuck in bad marriages.

At times, I think I also could have been one of those unfortunate women if I had succumbed to societal norms and pressure and continued living in a bad and violent marriage. Going against such norms takes great effort and has its own consequences. But if you manage to do that, then you are free. You might often find yourself alone in your fight, but nothing is more worthwhile than standing up for yourself.

For me, divorce was most liberating, as I was stuck in a bad and brutal marriage. For me, it was a blessing in disguise. And I find myself lucky to be in a country where I am free to opt for a divorce. Though people tried to convince me that divorce was a dead end and no future lay ahead of me, for me, it was just the beginning. While uncertain about my future, I found refuge in my work. Meanwhile, I found love a second time and remarried. Since then, it's been almost five happy years, and I am still counting.

My life may not have followed the ideal path of getting married by thirty, having kids, and having a settled career by thirty-five, but I can say that I feel content having chosen a path for myself as per my wish. I am thirty-six and happily married to a respectful and kind person. A year ago, I was privileged to have my debut poetry book published. And very recently, I left my well-established job to experiment with the uncharted waters of freelance writing and entrepreneurship. I co-own a creative firm named ArtLit, based in Chennai, and I love what

I am doing. I travel a lot, make new friends, and have fun with the old ones.

Though I have my ups and downs at times, life is overall good. Due to my traumatic past, I often feel fragile and anxious. But I make sure to work on my physical and mental well-being. And though leading an unconventional life makes me feel scared and lonely at times, it also gives me a sense of fulfilment that I am living life on my terms, doing and exploring what I have always wanted to do. So surely, swimming against the tide has its repercussions, but I believe you start enjoying the challenges if you are not forced to live up to someone else's expectations. The path is tough and uncertain, but my bruised past always gives me the hope that if I could survive what I had to, then I will do well in the future too, despite being on the wrong side.

*****

Author's Message

I hope my words bring some perspective to the subject of divorce and put it in a positive light. I hope that people begin to see divorce as a blessing in disguise rather than a curse if they are suffering and stuck in a bad marriage or situation, and I hope that my words bring solace to someone who is going through something similar, which is terrible, and simply does not want to give up on themselves or their lives.

23

THE RIGHTS TO SINDOOR

Uma Iyer

Every coin, every aspect, every situation, and every event in our lives have two sides. But more often than not, as humans, we have the tendency to focus on our side of the story first and then on the other, if only we have the opportunity, interest, and inclination for it. We see and feel what we want, especially when we are in the happiest or saddest phase of our lives. Being a woman, one of the worst or hardest things that I have seen happen to a woman is being deprived of all the privileges that a married woman enjoys, just because the woman has lost her husband to death, especially at a young age.

It takes just a day, a second, or a fraction of a second for death to knock on someone's door. But the echo of the knock is felt and heard by the woman for her entire life. This is the harsh reality of our society, a reality that I think I can share in this article through a real-life story.

Since Suman was a little girl, she used to visit the temple of Maa Durga every Friday. She was a favourite of everyone there, especially the priest, who used to love her the most. After the *aarti*, he would always give her a handful of *kumkum*.

Suman grew up and the priest witnessed her journey from childhood to before marriage, marriage, pregnancy, childbirth, and now as a single woman again after her husband died.

But now things stood changed. The first time she visited the temple after her husband's demise is a day she would never forget in her life. After the *aarti* got over, she was waiting as usual in line, but the priest just walked past her without giving her the *kumkum*. She should have expected it but was shocked, nonetheless. He even avoided looking at her later. On her return home, she cried and cried.

The other thing—or, should I say, the person—who changed immediately was her good friend. Her good friend's brother was engaged to get married, and Suman was already aware of it. As promised by her friend, Suman was supposed to be the first one to get the invite. Before the invite could be printed, Suman's husband passed away. And when the time came, Suman didn't get the invite at all. She knew the date of the wedding and expected at least a call from her friend but didn't receive one. Suman assumed that her friend didn't want to invite her. Maybe Suman had suddenly become inauspicious. The thought tore her apart, and she cried for several days after.

She no longer received the traditional *kumkum* and other married women's symbols that women exchange when they meet. Her own relatives treated her differently. She didn't get invited to rituals, which otherwise she would have been if her husband was alive.

Her experience got me thinking. Is the fact that her husband is no longer alive more important than the fact that she is still alive? Why can't she be treated the way she was before she got married? If she can be offered *kumkum* as a child or as an unmarried woman before marriage, then why not now? How does it matter if her husband is alive or not? She was an individual once; she is an individual now. Is *sindoor* only available to married women? Why do people who are surviving face the consequences of being survivors? Is a woman supposed to die first, before her husband, to get the respect a married woman gets? Do women lose their identity as individuals after their husband's death?

No! Definitely not! And this was just one side of the story. Suman's side. The side that makes us feel bad for Suman and the countless number of women who go through this discrimination every day.

But there is another side to the story! And the other side is a pleasantly surprising one. Suman loves her people, so she talked directly to them recently about why they treated her differently. After all, there is no problem that clear and honest communication between people cannot solve.

They gave her their side of the story. A story she didn't expect. After the temple incident, Suman decided that she would never visit the temple again. And she did not, until recently, when something made her do so. This time, when the priest came around after the *aarti*, Suman herself moved away. She approached the goddess's idol, where a small cup with *kumkum* was always kept. She took some, and when she turned around, she saw the priest standing there, smiling at her.

'Why are you smiling, Mama?' she inquired, amused. 'I'm glad you took it yourself,' he said, half sad, half happy. But Suman was not happy, though she pretended to be. 'What to do? You've stopped giving me on your own,' she said bluntly. 'Don't say this,' the priest replied, his heart broken. You are like a daughter to me. Please understand that when the temple trustees are around, I act differently. They are orthodox, you know that. I knew you were upset the last time; you were constantly looking at me. I did not have the heart or the courage to see you like this. 'I am sorry; I know you felt bad.'

Suman understood his actions and was grateful that he still loved her the same way. Suman's good friend was back in touch with her a few months after her brother's wedding. She never mentioned the wedding, nor did Suman ever ask about it, until one day she accidentally mentioned it. 'Don't mind. I just wanted to ask you, why didn't you invite me to the wedding?' And to Suman's surprise, her friend answered very honestly, 'Because I didn't have the strength to call you for marriage just when your own life and dreams had been shattered. I myself couldn't concentrate on the wedding. I knew if you would come here, all the elders in the family would have offered condolences and stopped you from performing any rituals. I couldn't see that happening. Your own cherished memories of your wedding would have come before your own eyes and would have made you upset. It was best if you didn't come since I wouldn't have been able to go against everyone openly at that time. I know how you must have felt. I cannot change the mindset of the people of that generation. That time, my silence was the best I could offer. But remember, I am always there for you. Sorry for the misunderstanding.'

'No. I am sorry that I misunderstood you all this time. Thanks for doing what you did for me. You stopped me from crying and grieving again and again.' Suman finally understood her friend's silence for all these months. Things are not always what they seem.

And finally, when Suman asked her own aunt the same thing, she got a very warm reply: 'It's not easy for me to see you like this. I have never spoken about your husband since that fateful day because I didn't want to evoke memories and make you cry. I thought seeing the kumkum would make you cry. I am sorry for the misunderstanding. But it was out of genuine concern. You may be strong and dealing with the situation well, but for us who are seeing you; it's not that easy to see our child like this. Next time, I will remember that you are strong enough not to get overwhelmed with memories. I now realize that you still like to be treated the way you used to be; for everything, by everyone. And only that can keep you truly happy.'

Suman understood her and her love and care. Suman's side of the story came out of her grievance. Their side of the story was out of love for her. And yes, Suman is strong; very strong.

It has been a year since Suman's husband passed away, and recently, Suman told me that some of her cousins and relatives did not wish her on her wedding anniversary, which just went by. Well, the death of a spouse does not erase the anniversary date from the surviving spouse's life. She did feel bad, but she knows that maybe they too have their side of the story.

But amidst all this, Suman has the support and love of her close family and friends, who still treat her without bias. Her mother-in-law stated firmly when Suman was crying after her incident at the temple, 'You don't have to wait for anyone to give you the *kumkum* in a temple. Simply go, take, and apply.'

Widowed women still have rights and still have freedom. Rights and freedom should be lived. She should enjoy this freedom.

*****

Author's Message

A widow has the right to sindoor and everything else, as long as she is alive. Just like every other woman, she is an individual with her own identity and life.

24

A SECURE MAN OR AN INSECURE HUMAN?

Swati Verma

From the moment a child is born, classification starts on the basis of whether it's a boy or a girl. A boy is associated with the colour blue and a girl with the colour pink. A boy is brought up one way; a girl is brought up another way. As they grow up, boys are trained to be a certain way, and so are girls. Just as girls are expected to be gentle, homely, delicate, caring, etc., boys are expected to be manly, outgoing, brave, skilled, etc., and these have been the conventions for years. These definitions are so concrete in the minds of people that any man or woman who doesn't meet these criteria is not well respected. It's only in the recent past that these distinctions have started to blur.

Men are taught to be manly from an early age. The definition of this term includes being rough, dominant, outdoorsy, masculine, brave, bold, hardy, etc. Even Google defines it so. So, any man who does not fit this mould is unfortunately stereotyped as gay or girly.

When a boy cries, he is told not to behave like a girl. If he is emotional and soft by nature, he is told to be a man. A boy cannot play with dolls or a kitchen set, while a girl can play with cars or guns and still not be ridiculed. A boy cannot wear shimmery clothes, while a girl can wear all the boy's clothes. For fun, if boys are dressed in frocks with makeup, parents will keep that photo, and relatives and friends will embarrass the boy by laughing at the photos. A boy cannot wear makeup or wear pink, and there are many other weird biases that society has set for boys. Hence, we often find boys applying any cosmetic cream, fairness cream, or moisturizer secretly, as they don't want anyone to find out about it. In metropolises where some men dare to do these things openly and love to stay up-to-date and fashionable, they are often termed "metrosexuals", who are basically a section of men who have similar interests as women and gay men. But even here, men who think they are very manly can't help but laugh at the metrosexuals.

We call our society a "men's society", but honestly, it's a "woman's world". All colours, glamour, and beauty are for her. She has the ability to live as both a man and a woman. But a man has to be a man all the time. If he depends on a woman, he is weak. If he is too busy at work making money, he is a bad husband or father. If he loves to cook and carry out domestic responsibilities, he is his wife's servant. If he is submissive by nature, he is spineless. There is an endless list of stereotypes about men that have existed for many generations. We mostly see the distress of women, and there is no denying that they have their own set of challenges. Being a woman, I can vouch for that. But a man has his own set of difficulties to face, as a lot is expected of him in society.

Laws all over the world are aimed at elevating and empowering women. Women have been looked upon as the weaker sex, but the truth is that men can't even dare to show their weakness, and hence, we as a society never realize how much we pressurize them.

When I look around me, I can see many men who are secretly facing this distress. They feel talking about it would make them look weak, and that is not manly. They are caught up in this web of masculinity that expects them to be always strong. I remember once, in a shopping mall, hearing a father scold his ten-year-old son as he was crying. He told him to stop crying like a girl and to be a man, and strong men don't cry. This is what has been fed into their minds since their childhoods. My neighbour's son, who stays at home unemployed and prepares for UPSC exams, gets to hear almost once a day how boys his age are independent and working, but he is still sitting at home and living off his parents' money. In financially backward families, an earning son is supposed to take care of his parents and get his sisters married. A son is expected to take care of his ageing parents. It's still a choice for the daughters if they want to do it instead.

Being part of the creative industry, I have seen many men face the crisis of instability. There is no guarantee of a next project once the current one ends. Sometimes even the payments we get for the projects are erratic. So the men who are married, have parents to support or have kids to send to school and work in the creative industries are always under immense pressure. One friend of mine is still fighting his divorce because his wife left him due to his unstable job and, being a woman, burdened him with domestic abuse and dowry cases. When a woman talks about domestic abuse, everyone believes her. But if a man did, people would laugh it off. How can we say we are building an even society by uplifting women when we also need to change the rules of manhood?

I see very few men who feel secure being completely themselves, even accepting the feminine qualities within them, just like a woman would boldly accept her masculine qualities and get applauded for it too. Men need to feel more secure, and that is only possible when we stop expecting them to be manly all the time and instead let them be humans all the time. Replace "manly" with "humanly" and teach the young boys to be just human, no man, no woman; only then could we build a more even society. A good human would be the most secure one, and I strongly believe there is no better way to make men feel more secure.

Secure men can eradicate a lot of social evils in society too. If a man feels a sense of security, only then can he support the women in his life. Otherwise, because he is easily intimidated, he will always try to crush the women who are stronger than him. My father-in-law once told me that women are very good managers, even better than men, and I believe only a very secure man can accept that publicly. My husband, too, like his father, is a very secure man who believes in the absolute equality of men and women. And that is why we are together in everything, be it domestic or financial matters. But an insecure man will not be able to handle a woman as smart as him. That is why, especially in our country, many women who are doing well for themselves end up divorcing because it becomes difficult for their partner to accept being any less. His manhood is called into question not only by him or his family but by everyone in society, whether through jokes or sarcasm, making him realize how much better his spouse is than him. A woman can accept her man being better placed professionally than her, but mostly a man can't, and it's society and its unfair expectations that make him this way.

Social evils like rape, domestic abuse against women, dowry, marital rape, acid attacks, divorces, and other social crimes would stop existing if men became more secure. Then they would not feel the need to suppress anyone to satiate their false sense of male ego and manhood. Many rapists have confessed that they couldn't take rejection from a girl and raped her in anger, a clear sign of an insecure man who is taught to be a man and take whatever he wants. If he accepts rejection, he will be weak, and his male ego cannot handle that. Another scenario was where an aunty in my parents' close-knit social circle was a victim of an acid attack, and she said the guy threw acid on her because she refused to marry him. But at the same time, there was this secure relationship between her and the man she was going to get married to, and he did not cancel the wedding because she did not look the same anymore. Her husband is an example of a secure man who did not ruin her life and sets a good example for other men in society.

So, let's ensure, as a society, that we stop stereotyping men based on this false sense of manhood and save them from growing into insecure men. Insecure men cannot let society grow; only secure human beings can. So be it man or woman; make them secure human beings. After all, there is a reason why a man's best quality is that he is a gentleman.

*****

Author's Message

Gentleness is so much a part of a man's identity as a good human being that no false sense of manhood should be allowed to ruin it.

25

DATE YOUNG BUT MARRY OLD

Niyati Singh

Our society has trillions of rules, which multiply when we start dating. So how did our community, which runs camps to normalize dating or marrying men younger than you, turn on dating a man older than you? Run through arranged marriages, and you will easily find an age difference that sometimes exceeds your average expectation. So how do we as a society play this game of double standards where if a man of older age dates a woman younger than him, we make a big fuss? So, what's the deal? Why are we undoing something our society has accepted in the fight to normalize older women dating younger men?

As I conversed with a couple with an age difference of seven years, they told me about their battle with the people beside them. The guy jokingly mentioned, 'People around her constantly nag her about being in a relationship with me.' And they went ahead and warned her that I might brainwash her. The girl laughed and continued his sentence by saying, 'It had gotten so bad that I doubted this relationship, but as we continued seeing each other, I knew this would work out despite our age difference.' As I talked with them for a few more hours, I questioned myself, 'What if they didn't dare to fight through the doubts people had instilled in them? What if the girl took people's advice to heart and didn't give this relationship a chance?' Then she might not have had the happiness that her face glowed in now, as well as the experiences and lessons she gained from this relationship. But most of the world might have missed out on a couple who came together like a missing puzzle.

Our world is covered quite a bit in shreds of hate, dislike, and other synonyms of these two words. What it needs right now is great love, care, and tenderness. If we keep the levels of these emotions as low as they are currently, we may create a dystopia. And I know achieving a utopia is hard, but it will make us create a dystopia. If dating a younger man is okay, then dating an older man should be okay too. We frequently discourage a woman from dating an older man, claiming that he may manipulate her or that it is paedophilia. But, when we want a woman to marry an older man, we say he will be mature, understand her problems, and do many other things. Then why don't we feel the same when dating a man older than her? What has changed in him? Except for the tag that says he is her boyfriend and not her husband. Why do we question the guy's integrity if nothing changes? If a person has to be wrong, it will not be affected by his age.

But the question is not only raised for the guy. The girl also faces the wrath of taunts and beliefs, especially if the guy is in excellent financial condition. She is often called a "gold-digger", a term that our society has only recently discovered. But often, people who tag the girl with this tag forget that a relationship cannot work if its existence is based on monetary benefit. Somewhere down the line in a relationship, as layers of personalities fade, one cannot stay with the other if it only started for money.

For any relationship to work, it needs love, care, and truthfulness. A lack of any of these guarantees the failure of a relationship and the commitment of two people to each other for the rest of their lives. As a society, we progress towards normalizing and de-stigmatizing particular things, we need to remember that in the process of de-stigmatizing, we are not creating new stigmas. It is a person's choice to date someone younger than him/her, just as it is another person's choice to date someone older than him/her. Two people can have different preferences, and we must support both ideologies. In protecting someone from a bad experience, we cannot stop them from experiencing the beauty that might come instead of what we assume will come. Take this as an example: Your ex is an ex for a reason. Did that stop you from choosing your present partner? No, right, it didn't make you assume that people sharing the same gender as your ex are similar to or clones of your ex. So how can we make assumptions about people who are older than us?

A man dating a younger woman is not always in pursuit of manipulating her, and a woman dating a man older than her is not always a gold-digger. They are none of the labels we have bestowed upon them as a society. They are two humans who connect, love each other, and are ready to travel miles and fight a billion problems to end up in each other's arms. If a man older than a woman loves her and a woman older than a man loves her partner, they will choose their partner in a room full of people because they both have something in common: love.

We often appreciate the marriage of two people, even though they share a vast age difference. As a society, we encourage women to find men older than them because we believe that it will lead to the fulfilment of the relationship. I don't know if age affects the fulfilment one feels in a relationship. However, if we can encourage marriage between younger women and older men, we can also be the advocates for their dating. Because the run-up to a wedding often starts with dating, if we don't let two people date, we can sometimes miss out on love stories that would swell up our hearts and make us believe that love is not dead. Age does not define the ability to find comfort in one's own arm; it is the energy that eliminates. And one can feel that vibe in anyone's arm; it doesn't have to be dictated by age, gender, or caste. If a woman can marry someone older, she can date someone older.

As I heard the couple's story (from the above conversation), I realized their love. The way they looked at each other and found comfort in each other, I could tell that he was in no way manipulating her, and she was in no way a gold-digger. The girl in between the conversations mentioned how maturity made her inner child feel safe and allowed her to bloom in the way she desired without worrying that he would judge her. As I was leaving, she told me about a time when she would be too scared of people's opinions while dancing, but with him, she was free, as if there was no one else in the room.

As I sipped on her words, I realized, isn't this what we say love has to be—somewhere one can feel safe? If someone seven years older than her could give it to her, then why not? Why shouldn't she be with that man? He was making her inner child feel safe, and I don't think I have seen a greener flag than this.

*****

Author's Message

The next time you label a relationship or even advise women about dating older men, remember that spending some time in both their companies might make you change your mind.

26

APPEARANCE ACCEPTANCE: THE RESPITE WE ALL NEED

Anuradha Gupta

William Shakespeare's "The Merchant of Venice" was part of our English syllabi in school. I recall how enamoured I was by the explanation given by my English teacher for "All that glitters is not gold". I memorized it verbatim. "The real value of a thing or person is not determined by their appearance but by their inner qualities". The words resonated deeply within me. They validated the values imbued in me by my parents, i.e., to be appreciated, one just needs to be good at what he or she does.

Cut to a few years later, when the movie *"Kabhi Khushi, Kabhi Gham"* got released. There was a dialogue: *'Mere saath prom mein jaane ke liye tum sab ko teen departments mein brilliant hona chahiye* — good looks, good looks and good looks.' ('To go to prom with me, you all have to be brilliant in three departments — good looks, good looks, and good looks.') When "Poo" said this in the movie, we all had a hearty laugh and loved her sass. Many of us, including me, even did a mock-up in front of the mirror with a little bit of extra spunk to mimic the iconic character. It was all fun and games until one day I realized I could read between the lines that in the real world, the inside doesn't always matter. Being a sizzle was more important than a steak in an appearance-fixated society.

To be a girl with a "short", "scrawny", and "mid-brown" skin tone and "dark circled" eyes in northern India is an invitation for a range of remarks and unsolicited comments from friends, acquaintances, and people in general. Since the comments never made much sense to me, I would smile, dismiss, and ignore them. But the irony is that the mind neither dismisses nor forgets. Impressible age combined with repeated instances breeds self-doubt and embarrassment. Furthermore, the mind stores memories associated with stressful situations more effectively, which has an impact on our self-confidence. Missing out on some good opportunities because of complexes has shown me that even the happiest and most confident people can be influenced by negative words. Happier and simpler were the days when, despite having a minimal wardrobe and a minimal understanding of the term "self-love", one used to be absolutely content and confident about their looks.

Ever wondered why there is madness around "looks"? Science seems to have a fair explanation for this. According to psychology, human beings have an inherent tendency to be drawn to things and figures that they deem aesthetically and visually pleasing. However, with every individual bringing their own emotions, experiences, and preferences to the world, there's a lot of subjectivity attached to what is "deemed aesthetically and visually pleasing". Perhaps that's why it's said, "Beauty lies in the eyes of the beholder". But why don't we delve deeper into the skin and character of the person? And how can one person's beauty and value be a derivative of another's vision? By that logic, I was never beautiful, whereas the fact of the matter is that we all are, irrespective of whether our beauty is acknowledged by a beholder or not.

For generations, there has been a pernicious mindset in which people feel better about themselves when they believe their outward appearance is "attractive" to "others". So, people indulge in self-grooming to fine-tune their look, which is great because anything that can make us feel good about ourselves without hurting others should be held in high regard. What is questionable, though, is when we do so to match the convention of attractiveness drawn in someone else's mind, keeping aside our individuality, style, and comfort.

During my growing years, I came across an extremely elementary yet significant concept that was centred on respect for fellow beings. As per that, the Supreme Being made all humans and living beings complete and perfect in every way, thus insinuating that "beauty" is not a subjective but an objective and absolute concept. So, it felt contradictory and annoying when I saw people judging others on the basis of their looks. It still does. But can we stop people from judging us? As a matter of fact, no!

Judging is an unconscious reflexive action of our brain that attempts to categorize our environment as good or bad, right or wrong, superior or inferior. Based on the stereotypes and notions pre-programmed in our minds, it computes and puts the above labels on people accordingly. So, when a person feels better or finds a boost to their own ego by finding a "fault" or, so to say, "a perceived shortcoming", which makes them label themselves as superior to the other, it is purely instinctive. However, what one doesn't realize is that such behaviour stems from their own insecurities, which they try to project onto others. For example, somebody pointing out a remark as personal as, 'How did you manage to pull off this bodycon with an unflattering chest and back?' would surely be fighting some demons of their own related to body image. This negative body image that one person inadvertently projects onto others because of the plummeting of their own self-esteem spirals into denting the confidence of both the judgy and the one being judged even more, and the vicious cycle continues. It is therefore the primary reason why we need to propagate the need for appearance acceptance right away.

The narratives have changed tremendously in the past few years, from the omission of "fair bride required" in the matrimonial ads to the inclusivity of our ideals as presented now by the media. However, there's still a lack of awareness and empathy, which often leads to disrespecting others unintentionally. A few months ago, I remember posting a full-length picture of myself wearing a dress. My social media account was soon flooded with multiple likes, positive comments, and messages from friends, followers, and alike. I was both amused and delighted. I wondered how much my younger self would have loved this overwhelming response because compliments earlier came my way with T&Cs. Not that much has majorly changed since then, because even now, when I meet people after a long time, some of them remark, 'You look great.' 'It's good you gained weight; you looked malnourished in college.' Phew! How on earth can one assume that they are complimenting me when they are completely invalidating how I looked in the past? Attractive bodies come in different shapes, sizes, and colours. But this mindfulness can emerge only if we accept and celebrate the people as they are.

Throughout our lives, we crave acceptance of different things from different people at different stages of life. And accepting yourself is the only way to avoid the crucifixion and people-pleasing. Even the mind needs to be trained better for being less judgy and more kind. But it doesn't come easy. In the last few years, I have consciously tried to stop worrying about what others might have to say; I am learning how to appreciate others without keeping looks as the focus. Also, journaling has brought some needed succour to the process by helping to get clarity of thoughts, declutter the mind, and bring better focus to my own life through positive affirmations. However, the most important step has always been to carry a smile to boost self-confidence. All of this together has led me to grow into a non-judgemental individual who not only protects her own peace but believes in seeing the core of another individual in a better light.

But body shaming won't stop with just an individual's behavioural change. It will require a structural process in terms of large-scale cultural and institutional changes because the initial two to three decades of any human's life will always be spent relying on external validation as it takes years to reach the maturity of loving oneself the way we are. So, it helps if every individual takes the onus to create a safe space for others by being compassionate and empathetic, both in terms of words and actions. For this, we all need to become changemakers who defy social norms of casual commenting and instead find ways to make people around us feel good about themselves because people don't just shine with makeup and clothes. They shine out of confidence and happiness. So, the next time you see a loved one struggling with body image, try genuinely complimenting them with words that see and laud beyond their physical beauty and share your light with them.

*****

Author's Message

I believe that body shaming knows no gender. Here's one of Rupi Kaur's quotes with a minor tweak for inclusion to fuel the movement for change: "I want to apologize to all the women and men. I have called them pretty and handsome before I've called them intelligent or brave. I am sorry I made it sound as though something as simple as what you're born with is the most you have to be proud of when your spirit has crushed mountains. From now on, I will say things like you are resilient or you are extraordinary. Not because I don't think you're charming, but because you are so much more than that".

27

SLUT-SHAMING GIRLS MUST STOP

Crrystal Agravat

Has any girl been teased or taunted because of the partners she slept with, or has any girl been taunted because of her past relationships? Has anyone assumed that dating a lot of men means having lots of sex? Then, I'm afraid to tell you that you are a victim of slut-shaming and that you should talk to someone right away because it can be mentally draining; it can have effects on your brain.

What is "slut-shaming"?

In the first place, let us unfold the blanket of the word "slut-shaming". Slut-shaming is the practice of condemning or reducing someone's (usually a woman's) worth based on their sexual reputation. It is the act of humiliating and degrading a girl or woman because of her sexual activity, which includes dressing in a specific manner, having sexual feelings, and/or discovering and displaying them. In simpler terms, it is a way of saying that "you are immoral or worthless".

Girls are viewed as objects that must be obtained in order to avoid hurting the male ego and turning dirty. Rape is caused by the breakdown of the male ego, as are domestic violence, cybercrime, sexual violence, and other forms of violence. The only distinction between men and women is in their genital organs. Unfortunately, society would not agree because men are considered superior to women, and they are expected to obey the man. The man's superiority strengthens his ego, and he expects not to be destroyed. Society is a community that comes with notions that distinguish people, but society can also come with notions that harm someone. Such an idea is ridiculous!

How does slut-shaming appear?

It can be extremely uncensored and demeaning to all victims. It can be explicit for some, mean for others, and psychologically damaging for still others. For some girls, slut-shaming can lead to a loss of self-esteem, and in the worst-case scenario, it can lead to depression. Depression can lead to girls committing suicide as they are judged based on their clothes, their sexual history, their relationships, and much more. Girls are targeted by a society that not only includes men but also includes women.

Types of slut-shaming

Slut-shaming is something that can be invisible and still cause harm. It has the ability to attract victims in such a way that one cannot deny it. To fully comprehend slut-shaming, different types of slut-shaming must be understood. Bullies and mean girls may picture the girls they aim for and then post crude or sexually explicit comments about their bodies on social networks. Abusers may also engage in pseudonyms and sexual harassment.

1. **In the form of images:** Slut-shaming is mainly done through pictures on social media. A teen may sometimes create an image of another teen that labels her a slut or shames her body in some way. For instance, in one case, teenagers made a series of Instagram pictures with captions and posted them to Instagram. One instance was a picture of a girl with exposed

cleavage and the caption, 'Hey girls, did you know that your boobs get in your shirt?'

2. **Sexting:** It is done in the form of texts and can result in slut-shaming. For instance, when a teen pair is dating, they may share explicit sexual or nude pictures. When they end the relationship, the frustrated partner openly embarrasses the other partner (usually a girl) by posting nude or partially nude pictures online. This type of behaviour is also ethically wrong and may result in charges of child pornography. In other cases, a teen may become obsessed with some other adolescent and send him/her seductive pictures.

Effects of slut-shaming

Double standards irritate many people. Boys are usually praised and admired for their sexual conquests, whereas girls are labelled as loose, easy, a slut, skank, or a whore. Victims of sexual abuse in any form may be more prone to anxiety, dangerous activities, and suicidality. In a similar manner, slut-shaming has also been linked to clinical depression, anxiety, and thoughts of suicide. Slut-shaming is not only verbally harmful but also mentally dangerous. The harmful effects that would result could be:

- Depression and anxiety
- Suicidal thoughts
- Self-harm
- Guilt and frustration
- Social isolation

Mental issues, like chain reactions, are a tool that can lead to other problems.

A similar incident happened to a close friend, and the way she was affected inspired me to write this article. (To protect her identity, her name is Anna.)

Anna had been a topper in her school years, but she had a disadvantage: She wore simple clothes that were not hip. Years passed before she received her offer letter from the United States. She decided to relocate to the United States to finish her degree. Because of her costume, she was excluded from her groups and labelled as "aunty", "nerd", "oily hair", and other derogatory terms were used to define her persona. Her self-esteem had been crushed, so she decided to undergo a makeover. The makeover did change her life, attracting male energy that could not be digested by her peers. She was once again the target of slut-shaming. Her nights would be made worse by anonymous texts at midnight offering her body and referring to her as a prostitute. Worse, her roommate, who had an inferiority complex, leaked her private photos. As a result of this, she was broken and went through a difficult time. Depression struck, she had panic attacks at school, and trauma issues followed her around like a pet puppy.

She would sit quietly in the room and not come out for days. Her parents were extremely concerned when they saw this. Her parents decided to devise a solution, creating a routine for her that included meditation sessions, phone calls with her grandparents, gym memberships, and a focus on eating a proper diet. Her mother used to follow Sadhguru, a mystical guru, and his principles, so she sent Anna to his hermitage for enlightenment. She was able to overcome her issues, accept change, and move forward with a new dawn after spending a few weeks at the Isha Foundation.

'I am able to breathe new air; I am born again, this time stronger,' she said after this magical experience.

What can be done?

Reading this far implies that you want to help your children, friends, or anyone else in the world, facing a similar issue. You have conquered the world. As a psychologist, one should always recommend therapy, but it can be expensive. However, there are some things that can be done without seeing a shrink. The first step would be to determine who is committing this heinous crime. Put on your detective glasses and pick up a magnifying glass. No, you just need to identify the criminal. If a family member is a victim, parents should always be on the side of their daughter or son. Supporting them would be an excellent measure, and simply listening to them would solve twenty per cent of the problem.

Parents should create a welcoming environment for their children, allowing them to come and talk freely without hesitation or barriers. According to research, teens or children who identify themselves as homosexuals are more likely to be slut shamed, so parents should be more accepting of their child's sexuality and preference.

This crime is the result of a societal difference. To fit the standards and avoid being degraded by society, the girl must dress up properly, whereas the boy is told that he looks handsome with a bare body and is a stud. This is an example of inequity that should be eliminated. Because rape is a crime, slut-shaming should also be considered a crime, and predators should be arrested. The victims can also face developmental and self-esteem issues, which in turn might lead to fatality.

Slut-shaming must be taken seriously in order to save our teenagers and our families. As parents and friends, we must communicate with anyone facing this situation, to give her a fresh start in life, and, most importantly, become a part of it. Communication is such a powerful tool that it can solve 99% of problems, and I have personally used it to heal myself of many issues. Communicate if you are facing such issues, and if someone in your family is facing such an issue, create a safe environment for her to let her express herself as a free bird.

*****

Author's Message

Make a worthwhile change.

Author's Message

Make a worthwhile change.

28

PERSPECTIVES OF MARGINALIZED INTER-CASTE COUPLES

Vinay Damodar

This article inquires about the problems faced and challenges overcome by couples who opt for inter-caste marriages. It also looks into the atrocity cases against Dalits and honour killings in the region of Maharashtra, where the target group is youth. There have been very few studies on this issue, which needs urgent attention.

There are very few researchers who have focused on this, and that is why there is very limited literature available on the issue. Very few have tried to explain the dynamics that work behind investigating honour killings and a huge number of other atrocities, especially in the case of inter-caste marriages and the experiences of inter-caste couples.

Dalits are classified differently in different parts of the country. In some places, it has to do with the occupation attached to it and the status given to Dalits. Below are some experiences shared by the inter-caste couples:

Twenty-six-year-old Raj Ganvir belongs to the Mahar caste and the Buddhist community. He married a Kumbi Patil (a woman of the dominant caste). He studied up to the twelfth grade and took up the job of a wage labourer for his earnings. He narrates his views on inter-caste marriage as follows:

'Before marriage, I was of the opinion that whenever I fall in love, I will not think about the caste identity of the girl and will marry whatever the caste of the girl might be. I don't have a problem with the caste. First of all, people should not look at caste, but if inter-caste marriage happens, they should not put a value on caste identity.'

Talking about the probable reasons for people's opposition to inter-caste marriages, he narrates:

'Due to inherent and rampant caste discrimination, people wish to arrange marriage within their own caste; they want to build relations within the caste. Most families oppose marriage outside their own society, and they wish that it should happen within their community; every parent wants their children to marry within their caste. Relatives taunt the families where inter-caste marriage happens. *Natevaik tomne martat* (Relatives were taunting me). And they are still doing so. Whatever we three couples have done in this area (inter-caste marriage), no one from our family or from society had said anything on that to us. There was no social outcry because only the older generation practised casteism. We (youths) do everything together nowadays. We all participate in the festive events of our society. We celebrate the Ganesh festival and organize and participate in all the festivals like the Mahadev Rally Festival, Boudh Pournima, Ambedkar Jayanti, etc. Friends from other castes and communities come together to celebrate and organize these festivals; even Muslims come.'

While expressing his views, he mentioned many things, including that he doesn't like arranged marriages, that for him caste was not a problem, and that he was ready to live life with a girl from any caste-related background. He also describes how the socio-cultural relations in his environment affect him. His views give us a picture of the current generation and show that the youth of the modern world does not give that much importance to traditional practices. They treat each other equally and without discrimination; they celebrate and enjoy festivals and organize events where inclusiveness for all other communities living nearby becomes a reality. In this manner, the principles of secularism and fraternity are also followed.

Rupesh Bundele, a thirty-two-year-old, who belongs to the Dhobi caste, studied up to the twelfth standard and later started working as a laundry man. He also does wage labour work for a private company. He got married to a *Khatik* (lower caste) woman. He says:

'At the beginning, people in a community see and treat the inter-caste couples as *Tuchhas* (lower-level beings). Nevertheless, if the relationship between the spouses lasts for a long time, people will change their perceptions about the couple and inter-caste marriage. People also see that arranged marriages within the same caste also break up. Contrarily, relationships formed in an inter-caste marriage last for a longer time. As there is opposition from society and family members to marriages of this nature, couples survive by having a mutual understanding as a support system for each other.'

Rupesh, when talking about his perceptions on inter-caste marriage, shared his views on how society or people look at inter-caste couples. They are looked upon in the same manner as poor people are, or, as we can say, as the marginalized sections are looked at: with low status and not with that much respect. He also shared the fact that arranged marriages are seen with respect and dignity. But he also points out that such respected and dignified arranged marriages also break up, whereas the inter-caste couples live together despite opposition from family and society. The bond between the boy and the girl becomes stronger, which gives them the strength to resist societal norms and the power to face people who oppose them.

He also shared the fact that a girl who marries outside her caste is seen differently by society and her family. He says that if the family members oppose inter-caste marriage, then society also takes the side of the family. What people in the society talk about the girl, who chooses inter-caste marriage, is explained in his words as follows:

'*Muline baherchya jatit lagna kele tar, samajatil loka ase mhantat gharchani sanskar nahi deu shakale, gharchani accept kela tar samaj accept karta. Gharcha virodh asla tar problem rahto.*'

This may be translated as follows:

'If a girl marries outside the caste, then people in society say to the family that they (parents) have failed to give proper socialization and discipline to their daughter. If a family member accepts the girl even after her inter-caste marriage, the society accepts them; if the family opposes, the problem persists.'

The respondent also makes some observations regarding accepting and resisting an inter-caste groom or bride based on his experiences. He says:

'People feel bad because, in cases of acceptance of inter-caste marriage, parents' names are lost. Parents have their own feelings, desires, and expectations of their children. As a result, when parents and family members discover that the person they are considering marrying falls short of their expectations, they attempt to reject them outright. Nevertheless, in cases where the bride or groom is rich and wealthy or in a higher job, such restrictions and opposition are at a minimum or absent. Money makes a difference. Status and position make a major difference.'

The respondent also narrates how and what inquiries the parents make in case any of their children tend to enter into an inter-caste marriage. According to him, a family may inquire about which community the person belongs to and how his or her behaviour is in general. In cases where the girl is from another caste or community, people tend to figure out only her probable mistakes. The respondent also made an important observation: *Ticha freedom la, ticha chukka mhantat.* This means that what we call the freedom of a girl to choose her life partner is, for others, nothing but her mistake (for going against the community tradition).

It is quite interesting to note the narrative of this respondent in that he talks of caste and class dynamics influencing the acceptance of inter-caste marriage. According to him, the nature and extent of people's reactions to inter-caste marriages are influenced by the caste and class of the other side. Sometimes, class is overvalued in accepting inter-caste couples. For instance, if a rich couple is engaged in inter-caste marriage, society doesn't say anything to them or does not look at the rich inter-caste couple in the same manner as they see a poor inter-caste couple. Every girl's family has expectations for her son-in-law, and if they get the boy of those expectations who is not from their caste, it takes less time for the couple to be accepted. And if the boy does not meet their expectations, they will make it an issue. In the whole process of marriage, the girl's position is very important; if she belongs to a lower caste or another caste, then her freedom (her behaviour) is seen as her mistake.

When couples face opposition from their families, their lives start from zero, and they become orphans. Here, we can see that couples are demanding jobs and a place to live. They believe that if they get the jobs, they will be financially secure and that any education they have received will not be wasted but properly utilized. While these couples have defied the false belief that inter-caste marriages are not permitted, they hope that in the future, the situation will change, and people will address the issue of caste and give greater acceptance to inter-caste marriages.

*****

Author's Message

A change in people's mindset with regard to inter-caste couples should definitely follow with time.

29

CASTIGATED

Dr Janki Mistry

India is a land of diverse cultures and identities. These identities have traditionally been based on community and caste. It is a prominent fact that the caste system of India is one of the oldest social stratifications in the world. It is as old as three thousand years[1].

In Hinduism, the four caste categories are: *Brahmins* (priests and teachers), *Kshatriyas* (warriors and rulers), *Vaishyas* (farmers, merchants, and traders), and *Shudras* (servants and labourers). These classes have been said to originate from the mouth, arms, thighs, and feet of a mythical character known as *Purusha*. There are other categories commonly referred to as Dalits, who are street sweepers and latrine cleaners, and Adivasis, the tribal people who came before the Dravidians and Indo-Aryans.

The caste hierarchy in India assumed a more complex shape, culminating in a system called "Chatuvarnya". This idea was further developed and strengthened by the British.

Dr B. R. Ambedkar has stated, *"If Hindus migrate to other regions on Earth, Indian caste will become a world problem"*. This statement reflects how divided we have become in the name of casteism and how we may infect the whole world with our mere entry and departure.

---

[1] *What is India's Caste System?* (2019, June 19). BBC News.

This line of thought is depicted in the matrimonial columns of the newspapers, where we intend to prioritize a bride or a groom of a certain caste as our family's choice. This deeply ingrained stigma does not end with a full stop in the newspaper's final paragraph.

This reality looks harsher at ground level. There have been real-life incidents where people belonging to lower castes have been denied water from wells. Practices such as refusing to eat food from the hands of a Shudra and violence against women of marginalized groups have come to the surface.

At a personal level, I have made interventions to end the popular school of casteism. My courageous voice has not always been met with acceptance and applause. In fact, it has been more of a conflicting situation, with heads nodding to say "no" to my out-of-the-box opinion.

There is a personal story that I would like to share at this point in time when I talk and write about casteism. Though the episode has ended, it will remain deeply etched in my memory.

A few years ago, my daughter was refused admission to a premier schooling institution in the city because I told them that I didn't belong to any caste—that I was casteless. I am unable to determine whether I did something wrong.

We were in the final stage of the admissions process. A form was supposed to be filled out and signed by both parents. We were made to sit in the kindergarten classroom on small little benches made for children between four and six years of age. There were about fifty parents and around twenty benches. So obviously, my husband, who under no circumstances would fit on the bench, was waiting in the corridor.

After I filled out the form, I went out into the corridor for his signature. One of the three staff members ran after me, hollering, 'Why did you take the form out of the classroom? Can't you see that other parents are sitting in the class and filling out the forms? If madam sees you with the form in your hand, she will scold us to no end. You people just don't understand anything.'

I looked at the form, wondering if there were any national secrets printed on it. However, my husband, who generally is a kind and meek soul and who refuses to enter into altercations, even with me, quickly came inside, took out his pen, and signed the form. Alas! The pen had black ink, and we were given strict instructions that the ink of the pen used to fill out the form must be blue. Thankfully, we were given some freedom regarding the shade of the blue colour.

The blackboard had explicit instructions regarding the way in which the form had to be filled out. Under the notion that I am an educated adult who had filled out umpteen forms up until the completion of my doctorate, I didn't bother too much with the instructions. So, instead of writing my surname, name, and middle name in that order, I wrote my name, my middle name, and then my surname, followed by my husband's name in the same way. I submitted the form to the staff member, who immediately brought me to my senses by tearing my form and reminding me that rules are rules for everyone and that I most definitely could not get away with writing my name. However, I was damn well pleased.

Up to this point, I had no objections. I had studied at the same school and was conditioned to obey the rules. But there was a field for religion and caste. Probably, I am a person greatly influenced by patriotic movies, so in the fields of religion and caste, I simply mentioned "HINDU". Of course, later on, my father corrected me and said, 'You should not even put Hindu. Just write Indian.' However, the madam concerned didn't like my answer, so she asked, 'Why have you written Hindu in caste too?' I told her that I always write Hindu because I don't believe I am anything else but that. But after that, as I iterated earlier, my form was dismissed, and I was promptly issued another form for hundred rupees.

I took the utmost care in filling out the next form in the best of my handwriting, fastidiously following the instructions on the board. I even wrote the date exactly as required (02-04-2012). My husband this time signed with the right colour, and again I went to the three staff members.

Another lady checked my form this time (the same one who had given me explicit instructions never to take the form out of the classroom). Everything was fine till she reached "CASTE".

Now you can imagine her plight, poor thing. She even had to check the apostrophe in the date. As a result, she clearly could not accept her inadequacy as a Hindu. So again, I told her that I don't write my caste anywhere. To which she said, 'How can that be? You must mention either the mother's or the father's caste.' My answer was that both our castes are different, so I don't know what my child's caste ought to be. I also told her that I have filled out many forms in many years, and nowhere has an objection of this sort been raised. *I said that I am neither a Brahmin, Vaishya, Kshatriya, nor Shudra.* I really can't write anything else. My tone may have been a bit stern by now. And now that I think of it, how foolish I must have sounded at that time! I was trying to ignore a system that even Gandhiji, in his lifetime, could not achieve success in eradicating.

Anyway, my form was submitted to the principal with a comment. So, when the three of us entered the principal's office, our greetings were reciprocated with angry eyes. We were told that they didn't want to have children whose parents behaved in this fashion. I was told that I was rude and that I should have more humility. I accepted all of this. Humility is a virtue I am trying very hard to inculcate, and hence I accepted the reprimand with all humility. But I still didn't accept that I had to write down my caste.

With a heavy heart and lots of doubts in our minds, we stepped out of the principal's office, my only child's birth certificate still in my hand. She was denied admission on the grounds that she had an overeducated, impudent mother who couldn't answer a simple question about her caste. She was denied the fundamental right to receive education by the school.

I have taken all this in a positive light. I am trying very hard to live in a secular fashion in a country that is mutilated by the caste system.

"Humanity is the religion of the brave". It is the light that we need to do away with the darkness of caste-made boundaries. It is much more beautiful, warm, and long-lasting. It unites, not divides. Today, I want to relinquish my caste in order to move towards this religion. Will I be able to do so?

*****

Author's Message

I am tempted to quote a few lines from Rabindranath Tagore:
"Where the mind is without fear and the head is held high,
Where knowledge is free,
Where the world has not been broken up into fragments by narrow domestic walls,
Where words come out of the depth of truth,
Where tireless striving stretches its arms towards perfection,
Where the clear stream of reason has not lost its way into the dreary desert sand of dead habit,
Where thee leads the mind into ever-expanding thought and action,
Into that heaven of freedom, my God, let my country awake".

30

GIRL CHILD LABOUR: AN OUTCOME OF EDUCATIONAL DISCRIMINATION

Juhi Arya

The International Labour Organization (ILO) established "World Day Against Child Labour", which is marked annually on June 12th. This day, instituted by the United Nations (UN), brings attention to the plight of child labourers around the world and the need for a concerted effort to end all forms of child labour. It is the objective of the ILO to eliminate child labour by 2025. In relation to this goal, much work needs to be done. Every child deserves a peaceful and secure childhood, along with the chance to go to school. Unfortunately, these essential rights are still being denied to 63 million[1] girls around the world who are engaged in child labour, many of whom are suffering from the worst forms of child labour.

Children, or child labourers, are a heterogeneous social group. Education for a child is the primary ladder towards obtaining decent work and a livelihood as an adult. The organization "Free the Children" defines child labour as work done by children below the age of fourteen, which restricts or damages their physical, emotional, intellectual, social, or spiritual growth as children. There is little documentation on girl child labour, which can also be seen as

---

[1] (n.d.) Retrieved from https://www.antislavery.org/wp-content/uploads/2017/01/discriminationpaper.pdf

evidence of the invisibility attached to her labour, though it contributes so widely to the family, community, and society at large.

The situation of the girl child labourer is particularly alarming due to the gender discrimination prevailing on a large scale at various societal levels in India. This fact induces parents to value their daughters less than their sons because they will not be a source of economic support when the parents become old. This is once again linked to the fact that the probability of girls being sent to school is lower in comparison to boys. Girl child labourers face multiple disadvantages such as rampant discrimination, physical and mental harm, sexual and economic exploitation, or even death. By taking up work like childcare, cooking, and cleaning, girls have to combine long hours of household chores with some form of economic activity outside the household, imposing a "double burden" on young girls. This can have a negative impact on any opportunity for school attendance and can cause expected or unexpected physical harm to girls.

Girls may often be the last ones to be enrolled and the first ones to be withdrawn from schools if a family has to make a choice between sending a boy or a girl to school. Girls' access to education may also be limited due to other factors, such as the safety of the journey to school or the lack of adequate water and sanitation facilities on school premises. Without access to quality education, girls shift into the labour force at an early age, well below the minimum age of employment.

Research has proven that educating girls is one of the most effective ways of tackling poverty. All the factors that contribute to child labour were pre-existing and have been exposed and amplified.

The census of India 2011 reports a total of 10.1 million working children in the age group of five to fourteen, out of which 8.1 million are in rural areas, mainly engaged as cultivators (26%) and agricultural labourers (32.9%)[1]. There are a lot of side effects of working at a young age, which include the risk of contracting occupational diseases like skin diseases, diseases of the lungs, weak eyesight, tuberculosis (TB), etc.; vulnerability to sexual exploitation at the workplace; and lack of education. These children who grow up are unable to avail themselves of development opportunities and end up being unskilled workers for the rest of their lives. The constitutional and legal provisions associated with child labour are mentioned in Article 23 of the Indian Constitution, which says that any type of forced labour is prohibited. Article 14 states that a child under the age of fourteen cannot be employed to perform any hazardous work. Furthermore, Article 39 states that "the health and strength of workers, men and women, and the tender age of children are not abused, and that citizens are not forced by economic necessity to enter vocations unsuited to their age or strength". In a similar manner, the Child Labour Act (Prohibition and Regulation) of 1986 prohibits children below the age of fourteen from working in hazardous industries and processes. Policy interventions such as MGNREGA 2005, the Right to Education Act 2009, and the Mid-Day Meal Scheme have paved the way for children to be in school, along with guaranteed wage employment (unskilled) for rural families. Moreover, with the ratifications made in 2017 in International Labour Organization Conventions No. 138 and 182, the Indian government has demonstrated its commitment to the elimination of child labour, including that of those engaged in hazardous occupations.

Challenges Faced by Girls

In a publication titled "Child Labour, Global Estimates 2020 ", the ILO highlights trends that show that out of 160 million children involved

---

[1] Organization, I. L. (2009). Retrieved from
https://www.ilo.org/ipec/Campaignandadvocacy/wdacl/WorldDay2009/lang--en/index.htm

in child labour, 39% are girls. However, this figure does not include household chores done in children's own homes.

Girls in child labour are more likely to be in services, including domestic work, which is generally underreported. Domestic work, including work in third-party households, is a form of child labour that is usually hidden from public view and lies beyond the scope of labour inspectorates, leaving girls especially vulnerable to abuse. When the definition of child labour is expanded to include household chores lasting 21 hours or more each week, which are classified as hazardous, the gender gap in prevalence among boys and girls aged five to fourteen years is reduced by almost half. Worldwide, 7.1 million children are engaged in different forms of domestic work that constitute child labour. Of these, 4.4 million (or 62%) are girls, and 2.5 million (or 57%) are aged between five and eleven years[1].

Measures to Prevent Female Child Labour

- Enact explicit laws and put in place enforcement mechanisms and child protection interventions to counter the risks faced by all children, but especially girls, engaged in domestic work.

- Implement community-based dialogue, social and behaviour change interventions, and parenting programmes to help counter unequal gender norms.

- Implement cash transfers and other social assistance programmes designed to diminish financial barriers and improve quality education and learning for girls.

- Increase the number of flexible learning paths available so that all girls can benefit from high-quality education and pursue an education that leads to more equal employment opportunities in all sectors, including science and technology.

---

[1] The Hindu

Women can play a crucial role in the fight against child labour. Let's examine some approaches that can make a difference.

When women are educated, their children are less likely to be involved in child labour and hazardous work. By improving the literacy and numeracy skills of women, poverty is reduced, which is one of the main drivers of child labour.

Empowering women economically is another powerful means of reducing child labour. When women can generate income and are provided with greater access to finance to start or grow small businesses, the impact on communities, especially children, can be transformative. When women can generate additional income, families can be lifted out of poverty, and children are more likely to stay in school. Additional income also helps families better deal with shocks, such as the ongoing COVID-19 pandemic and mitigates the need to rely on children for labour.

Women should be actively and equally involved in child labour eradication programs. For example, when more women are employed as child labour monitors, monitoring programmes improve. Without the leadership and commitment of women to the cause of ending child labour, they are doomed to fail from the outset. When women are provided with the support and means to take decisions on behalf of their families, children are less likely to drop out of school and become involved in child labour.

The European Union (EU)[1] is already committed to taking action to support gender equality through international cooperation. To help eradicate child labour, the EU is promoting wider access for women and girls to quality education and skills and creating decent jobs and income-generating activities for women. Expanding social protection systems and improving legal frameworks, while considering the specific country context and situation of women and girls, are also

---

[1] Union, E. (2021). Google. Retrieved from https://international-partnerships.ec.europa.eu/news-and-events/stories/empowering-women-and-girls-end-child-labour_en

part of the EU's actions. One such example is implementing the EU-funded CLEAR Cotton project in Pakistan with the International Labour Organization and the Food and Agriculture Organization (FAO). The project has been implemented for cotton-growing communities and to empower women to reduce child labour.

They conducted a study with the Punjab Economic Research Institution (PERI) on "Gender Roles, Related Work Burden, and Their Effects on Child Labour in Agriculture in Punjab". The research demonstrates the clear link between child labour and the distribution of tasks and responsibilities at the farm and household levels, which have different implications for boys and girls.

The work burden of the whole family is dependent on three crop cycles per year; however, the limited income from the same crops does not allow for investment in more profitable and stable revenues or the education of children.

That is why FAO is assessing the agri-food market to identify viable economic opportunities to implement income-generating activities for women in small-scale farmers and households. Women will be trained to form social cooperatives or self-help groups (SHGs) and accompanied by them to invest in children's education.

*****

Author's Message

Women and girls must be at the centre of all solutions for the eradication of child labour!

31

PLIGHT OF NORTH-EASTERN MASSES IN MAINLAND INDIA

Bhumika Kukreja

The north-eastern states of India, which are in a paternalistic way called the "Seven Sisters of India", are a beautiful land of people living in a fabricated anonymity of unknowns in mainstream India. The states of Arunachal Pradesh, Assam, Manipur, Meghalaya, Mizoram, Nagaland, Sikkim, and Tripura are an unexplored paradise brimming with greenery, wildlife, and a sphere of beauty to behold. But unfortunately, this beautiful part of our country lags in terms of development, resources, and opportunities, with a major segment of people moving to bigger cities each day to explore more career paths.

'Do you eat rice?' 'Do you consume the meat of dogs?' 'Are momos part of your staple diet?' 'Do all of you take drugs?' Such are the questions that puzzle and disrespect the north-eastern diasporas in other parts of the country. And these things continue.

A nineteen-year-old boy was killed in a street brawl. Nido Taniam, from the state of Arunachal Pradesh and a student at the Lovely Professional University in Punjab, was on holiday in Delhi. He stopped at a market to ask for directions. Shopkeepers thrashed him, and the next day he died of his injuries. People were so callous that they couldn't stop themselves from characterizing the boy's mongoloid features and labelling him Chinese. This was not the first time that news of racial discrimination against the north-eastern masses raised questions about the country's ostensibly "Unity in Diversity" image.

In 2009, nineteen-year-old Ramchanphy Hongray from Nagaland was murdered by a student from a prestigious technology institute for protecting herself and resisting rape. Another incident arose when a girl from Nagaland was brutally raped in Delhi. And the irony is that the girl herself was blamed. Police officials as well as members of the public advised the girls to stop partying and behave themselves in order to stay safe. The whole story was knitted against them, and the girl was presumed to be characterless based on the fact that she hailed from a north-eastern state of the country.

In 2012, Richard Loitman, a nineteen-year-old student of architecture who hailed from Manipur, was found dead after he was assaulted by his college seniors in Bangalore. The same year, Dana Sangma from Meghalaya, who was an MBA student at a reputed university in Noida, committed suicide after being accused and humiliated for cheating in exams.

Out of the lakhs of people moving to mainland India from the north-eastern states, the majority of them have been subject to several kinds of humiliation because of their appearance; they have faced discrimination at some point or another. According to surveys, the majority of them do not feel included even when they hold an equal or higher position in a group. People have been made to feel that they are not important. They have been discriminated against based on their looks, language, accent, lifestyle, personal choices, and what have you.

The Indian Council of Social Science Research did a study during the COVID-19 phase. According to the study, young people from the north-east face bias in cosmopolitan cities. Problems come in the form of being forced to eat in stalls run by their community members; rented rooms are also not easily available.

Whatever the situation, the most pitiful condition is that the problems of the north-eastern communities, such as cultural discrimination, refugee influx, identification issues, intra-state boundary disputes, political incursions, a lack of infrastructure and affordable connectivity to mainland India, and so on, have never worried anyone in society and have always taken a back seat in the list of social causes. That part of the country is always ignored and is one of the lowest on the priority list. Due to these issues, these states are not able to grow at a pace similar to other big cities, and hence, youth are forced to move out to other places. But unfortunately, they are not accepted in these big cities and face unethical thrashing at times.

Racial discrimination, which is carried out on an everyday basis, may not be very apparent, but ignoring its existence has caused problems in the past that continue in the present. Cases come into the spotlight when famous celebrities like Shilpa Shetty are discriminated against in a foreign land. But when it comes to discrimination against people in their home country, the issues are only acknowledged when some tragic incident takes place, most probably one involving a death.

Big, developed cities lay bait for the north-eastern populations in terms of infrastructure, lifestyle, education, growth, and job opportunities but lag on being sensitive, showing respect, and creating an environment of inclusivity and emotional support.

The north-eastern masses have been chastised for their liberal dressing, food, and lifestyle, which is allegedly considered an outside activity by the society's so-called learned population. Alas! Perpetrators who condemn such discriminatory acts just have their intolerant attitude as a justification.

Stereotyping is rampant in India. Women from the north-east are seen as morally loose and easily available, while men are painted as losers, drug addicts, or insurgents. Racism is not a newly cultivated disease. It has been prevalent in India in different forms and is still there, hiding itself behind the veil of superficiality that comes with urbanized India.

Stereotypical beliefs about race, gender, lifestyle, and the refusal to accept the identities of others have accumulated over time to form a package of malice that has rotten our society. It should not be surprising if we find all these ideas near us, but it should definitely be alarming for their assumed "invulnerability", which has caused damage beyond repair. Authorities alone cannot be blamed. Laws are important, but more important is following them.

The majority of the emphasis should be placed on those vultures that have eaten our humanity and made us so angry about how we treat others that killing or harassing is just another act.

The whole idea lies in the mentality of people and being open to accepting diversity, not only at the superficial level but at the root level. People should be accepted the way they are and treated in the same way as everyone else. Discriminating against someone solely on the basis of their appearance is not only unethical but also illegal. Treating someone as an outsider in their own country is just like treating a family member as a stranger in his own home. People from different places and states are bound to have different features, characteristics, and choices. People should be sensitive enough to make others feel included and create a mentality in which everyone is treated as an equal and no one is an outsider. Although we should have understood this long ago, it is high time that the country considers this an important issue, and everyone is treated as one and not as an outsider in their own country.

*****

Author's Message

Nobody in their own country should be treated as an outsider, let alone just on the basis of their looks. Every living being is a gift of God and should be embraced in the best possible manner.

32

LGBTQ+ GOT A CURE

Niyati Singh

We live in a society where being LGBTQ+ is assumed to be a disease. Material progress has done nothing to advance our thinking. So, to accept people and their choices that are not in alignment with the laid-out thoughts is a huge task. When we experience something different than what we would consider normal, we start tagging it as foreign, and in the case of LGBTQ+, we tag it as a disease.

How do you cure a disease? The answer is simple: You go to someone who knows his way around it. So prominently in India, these "disease cures" are found in *tantriks, babas,* homophobic doctors, and whatnot. These *babas* perform something we call "conversion therapy", an assumed way to get rid of Satan that has caused a person to find his or her place in the LGBTQ+ community. However, hidden behind the two words used to describe this process is a mannerism that can make you shiver and break. It is a nerve-wracking process where the person goes through intense mental and physical abuse. These sessions leave a person doubting his/her decisions and believing he/she is wrong in being unique.

But what forces people to subject their loved ones to this conversion therapy? The need to fit into the conventional standards put down by society. This makes people believe that anything that doesn't fit into this so-called normal is to be looked at through various lenses of doubt and question. But are all the lenses, right? Is it possible to fail by refusing to conform to societal stereotypes? Or does it guarantee the right to subject oneself to pain?

Though we know the answers to all the questions above, we still fail to wash away the dull colour that societal stereotypes have laid on us. Our failure to eradicate it is the root cause of the thriving business of *babas* and *tantriks*. For a venture to prosper, you need customers. Where and how do you find the customers? The answer might seem dumb because the answer is that you need to explore your target market. And it is the thought process and the societal norms that have enabled the creation of this market. It is leading to the modern age of the gas chamber, a chamber that doesn't kill you physically but haunts you as you navigate your life. Those who live after this experience, doubt their choices and the people around them.

Conversion therapy involves various medical and faith-based methods. But is it consensual, which is the main worry? Often, it is the one into which you are draped without being asked about your wants. To go through something that inculcates a tremendous process of moulding you into believing that your choices and thoughts are incorrect and not in sync with whom you want to be is often a test of one's confidence, inner peace, and beliefs. But if we combine this tasking process with forcefulness and the absence of consent, we are inflaming the process of creating a broken and shattered person.

The urge to find our place in society has fuelled the growth of these conversion therapy clinics. It has allowed these self-proclaimed society mentors and revolutionists dressed as *tantriks* and *babas* to build a successful business based on human emotions, to break those clients, and to plant a seed of doubt in their minds. But a fundamental question that we often look past while acting from a place of stereotypical thought is, where is this leading us? Is it contributing to our present or our future? Not every decision you take has to contribute to the present or future. However, this is only true if you act on your decision without regard for societal stereotypes. As soon as the societal stereotype factor steps in, become wary of what you immerse yourself in. Inquire because, more often than not, the world around us has no idea about us or our loved one's well-being. They assume and presuppose things on a mass basis. But we are not a herd of sheep. We are humans. Each of us carries within ourselves a vast depth of emotion and understanding. One wrong step towards our complexities can lead to a disaster that the world is not ready to embrace and accept.

This mass problem stems from a tiny phrase one often hears as a kid. No guesses. That line is, "What will people think"? A conscious eradication of it from your child's childhood might help your child grow into someone who decides upon matters while keeping the other person and their own emotions at heart. It is important to remember that love and care for someone are both positive emotions. Our world's brim has an enormous bundle of hatred and jealousy. It might do well if streams of love flow into it. Then the world might be a more liveable place, and we would experience a world that is not killing us anymore.

We have no control over how we feel about someone. It is our feelings that control it. How we look, feel, and embrace ourselves can be unique and different. No divine power has stated that a body is supposed to look this way or that a person can only feel this way. Each individual is made of different chromosomal combinations, DNA, and genetics that account for and explain why he or she might be different. So why do we need conversion therapy? The feeling that we believe stems from the presence of Satan is a personal choice and one that makes someone happy. No amount of conversion therapy can help someone get rid of how he or she feels or what his or her body is like.

Out of 100 people subjected to conversion therapy, 98 reported[1] that it caused them psychological or physical damage. These shops,

---

[1] Minj, N. (2022, September 14). The horrors of queer conversion therapy in India. Scroll.in.

which are very popular in countries such as India and Pakistan, can often be found among the street shadows. Standing amidst various stores, these are often unrecognizable, and you often find yourself walking past them until and unless you are searching for them with a lamp in your hands. Then you become well aware of the exact location in which you would find this shop, and you might even have your way with the guy doing that job. Because your well-wisher would have not only given you a briefing on the shop's directions but would have gone an extra step by calling this shop's persona and informing them about your visit with your loved one. Yeah, the same loved one whom you cannot accept as he or she is; so next time you call him or her your loved one, question yourself: Are you considering him or her to be your loved one if you cannot even accept him or her as he or she is?

It's high time we look past people as broken just because we feel they are damaged or imperfect. Making someone feel inadequate about their choices is today's form of electrocution. Remember that sometimes people do not require assistance because, if they chose this for themselves, they would have given it considerable thought and even considered how they do not fit into society's norm of "ordinary".

*****

Author's Message

Remember! They don't need you to look out for them this term. They need your support, and you should stop finding a cure for LGBTQ+.

33

HUSH! IS SOMETHING WRONG?

Karen

Often, people who are a little different from others are looked down upon, belittled, or judged. This leads to a feeling of inferiority and fear in the minds of these differently abled people. Mental health includes our emotional, psychological, and social well-being. It affects how we think, feel, and act. We hear about mental health problems but are unable to find the courage to do anything about them, so we stay quiet. On the contrary, one should go to a psychologist for help. So that they can advise you on making better decisions in life.

Nowadays, people frequently disregard mental health symptoms such as depression, hypertension, anxiety, slow learning, and learning disabilities. Since many people are not aware of it, they think that counselling from a psychologist is not important.

But getting the right help from a psychologist will help these people, in the long run, to think better for themselves and make better life decisions. So, taking advice from other people is not wrong. On the contrary, getting the right advice and guidance can change a person's life for the better. Since taking counselling for mental health is advisable, you can share anything you feel like with the counsellor: thoughts, feelings, worries, anxieties, etc.

If timely action is not taken, mental health can cause a slew of problems or lead to suicidal tendencies, particularly among young people. So, it is of the utmost necessity that we create awareness about mental health. People need to understand that a person with mental health problems is not abnormal, but he or she does need a little love, guidance, care, and support. But most importantly, such people need to be accepted by society without bias.

A **mental disorder**, also known as a mental illness or psychiatric disorder, is a pattern of behaviour or thought that causes significant distress.

A **learning disability**, learning disorder, or learning difficulty is a condition in the brain that causes difficulty comprehending or processing information. It can be caused by several different factors, like malnutrition, stress or tension experienced by the mother during pregnancy, etc.

Dyslexia is a learning disorder that involves difficulty in reading due to problems in identifying sounds of speech and learning how they relate to letters and words (decoding). It is also referred to as a "reading disability". It is a result of individual differences in areas of the brain that process language.

Dysgraphia is a learning disability that affects writing abilities. It can manifest itself as difficulties with spelling, poor handwriting, and trouble putting thoughts on paper.

Dyscalculia is a learning disorder that affects a person's ability to do math. Much like dyslexia disrupts areas of the brain related to reading, dyscalculia affects brain areas that handle math and number-related skills and understanding.

Anxiety is an emotion characterized by feelings of tension, worried thoughts, and physical changes like increased blood pressure.

Depression (major depressive disorder) is a common and serious medical illness that negatively affects how you feel, the way you think, and how you act.

A **slow learner** is a child of below-average intelligence whose thinking skills and scholastic performance have developed significantly more slowly in comparison to his or her age. Slow learners are learners whose learning pace is slower than their peers.

Poor mental health makes us more vulnerable to certain physical problems, such as heart disease, high blood pressure, also called hypertension, a weak immune system, gastrointestinal problems, obesity, and early death.

For students specifically, mental disorders can affect their classroom learning in ways such as poor attendance, difficulties with academic performance, poor social integration, trouble adjusting to school, problems with behaviour regulation, and attention and concentration issues.

Women who are abused are also more likely to develop depression, anxiety, and eating disorders. Domestic violence can lead to serious mental health issues such as depression or anxiety, as well as physical health issues like heart disease and respiratory problems. Domestic violence can leave you depressed and anxious and increase your risk of having a drug or alcohol problem. Women face a lot of stress due to early marriage, dowry, domestic violence, etc., but they face it and manage it very well by seeking help.

Child abuse includes physical, emotional, and mental abuse, as well as neglect. Dealing with abuse can leave you feeling confused, scared, or exhausted. A child who is abused is more likely to abuse others as an adult so that violence is passed down from one generation to the next. We have to overcome all odds in life. Counsellors, family, and friends can assist you in sorting through all of the emotions associated with abuse.

Mental health can also be affected by peer pressure, wherein we tend to unnecessarily compare ourselves with our friends.

Stress is also a part of mental health. Relationship stress can increase levels of the stress hormone cortisol, which has been linked to various mental health issues.

Chronic depression, anxiety, and personality disorders are all linked to cardiovascular diseases such as coronary heart disease, hypertension, heart attacks, and obesity. Impotence and premature ejaculation are two examples of sexually dysfunctional problems. Men may be more likely to react with the fight-or-flight response under stress compared to women, who show more of a pattern of tending towards and befriending. This increases men's susceptibility to high levels of stress during certain situations when compared to women. Stress affects us all. You may notice symptoms of stress when you have to meet deadlines at work, manage your finances, or cope with a challenging relationship.

Anxiety is your body's natural response to stress. Face your fear if you can. If you always avoid situations that scare you, you might stop doing things you want or need to do. Difficult experiences in childhood, adolescence, or adulthood are a common trigger for anxiety problems. A big event or the build-up of smaller stressful life situations may trigger excessive anxiety—for example, a death in the family, work stress, or ongoing worry about finances. People with certain personality types are more prone to anxiety disorders. Women are more likely than men to take charge of their stress and manage it well.

Mental health is taken for granted these days. No one wants to seek help at the right time because they feel that society may not accept them. But seeking timely help is important to reduce mental health problems. People in the olden days were not aware of their mental health issues and did not know where to address them, so they lived with them. But today, it is possible to take advice and live a stress-free life.

Counselling is a two-way street between the counsellor and the client. Professional counsellors help clients identify goals and potential solutions to problems that cause emotional turmoil; seek to improve communication and coping skills; strengthen self-esteem; and promote behaviour change and optimal mental health.

Activities such as sports, gardening, dancing, cycling, walking the dog, cleaning, or going to the gym, for example, are great ways to improve your mental health.

Mental health awareness is the need of the hour. Poor mental health is a risk factor for chronic physical conditions. Mental health affects how we think, feel, and act. It also helps to determine how we handle stress, relate to others, and make choices. Mental health is important at every stage of life, from childhood through adolescence and adulthood. Mental health awareness is an important initiative to improve understanding of mental health conditions and increase access to healthcare for those who need it.

The mental health awareness camps will guide you on how to overcome stress, depression, and other mental health problems. They will teach you how to remain calm in stressful situations like hypertension. Even slow learners can get help from the camp. We have to face our difficulties in life and overcome them. So, take advice from the counsellors and follow up with them throughout your life. Some people think that taking help is not important, but even they can join the mental health camp to learn more about their problems and get timely help. Taking the right advice from the right person is always important.

Men face a lot of work-related stress, but instead of seeking help, they take it out on women, which is not right. People should attend mental health camps and try to solve their problems.

Even in modern times, many women and men still remain silent, fearing the outcome. But due to the mental health camps, many people have come out to seek help.

So, in today's world, almost everyone has issues and faces problems at some point in their lives, but the courage and determination to overcome your problems are essential, and you should seek help rather than bear them silently.

*****

Author's Message

Dear friends, in most cases, a mental illness won't get better if you try to treat it on your own without professional care. If you need help, stand tall, seek it, and break false conventions related to mental illnesses.

34

SUPERSTITIONS—GAMES OF THE MIND

Swati Verma

A soul leaves a body after death, but does it also leave behind the memories of this lifetime, the relationships with children, siblings, grandchildren, and all dear ones? People say the soul is neutral, but does that mean total detachment from everything it built while it was in the body? Now that it is looking to find a new body to reside in, does it try to harm even loved ones if they cross its path? Is a soul that technical or devoid of emotions?

All these questions arise when we hear about the death of a loved one. The mystery of the afterlife gives rise to many such theories. The elderly have their own set of beliefs; the pundit narrates the *Garuda Purana* every day, which talks about the journey of the soul. Science and books each have their own set of ideas and research. But our generation refuses to believe many such things because there is no logic to most of these theories. We are a generation of facts and figures, not a generation of stories and superstitions.

But one gets shaken up when one takes a step against these beliefs to break them, and something inexplicable happens. This is about a night that is such a mystery and an experience I may never forget. There were many theories and explanations I got from everyone the following day when I told them the happenings of this mysterious night. But I could clearly see that none of us had any clarity on the afterlife journey of a soul.

As our elders say, the soul is said to be in a state of unrest for about thirteen days until it finds another body. As a result, people who live in the house where the deceased lived must be cautious not to intrude on the territory of the soul.

The loss of a loved one—my grandmother—and seeing her ice-cold body lying in front of me stripped of all her worldly possessions was a sight I can never forget. We dressed her in fresh clothes, decorated flowers all over her, carried out all the necessary rituals, and mourned her loss. I just wanted to remember her fondly, as the last memory of us together in that same room was a good one. She was feeling much better from her illness, and after months, she could speak like this. We spoke for almost three hours, and she sounded so much better. I wanted to remember only that and not what I was seeing in the present day. The active, restless soul she was, being so lifeless, did not agree with her. I stayed in her room and shed a few tears. Then we bid her goodbye.

Everyone was now preparing for the thirteen-day journey to help the soul move to its next life. The rituals kept us busy all day. And in the evenings, everyone tried to be normal and happy because they said departed souls were watching and it hurt them to see us in pain. I understood all of this as it only created positivity, and I believed rules that spread happiness need not be unnecessarily questioned. But later that evening, I still sat in my grandmother's room and told my mother we would sleep here today. An elderly relative who came from a village far away warned me that this was a bad idea. Even the room where the soul died is to be preserved. I politely told him it was my grandmother, and she would never harm me. I don't believe in rules that spread fear and negativity.

My worst mistake was ignorance and total disregard for any rules that had no explanation. All I knew was that my grandmother had died, and she had loved me and could never harm me. I wanted to stay close to her belongings, to places where she rested, and to anything that stayed with her till her final days. But little did I know that, unknowingly, I was invading the space of a disturbed soul, looking to settle in another body.

After spending a whole day at the spot where she mostly stayed in her final days and where she finally lost her life, I slept there at night too. I woke up to a chill passing through me at 3:00 a.m., as I had checked the time then. I thought I was just cold due to the weather outside, and I covered myself well with the blanket. Winter nights are really difficult sometimes, as I unconsciously throw away the blanket in my sleep. As a result, my sleep is frequently disrupted. It was just the beginning. I felt something different inside me, like a push or something trying to move me away from that spot.

I freaked out and shifted to the other side immediately and hugged my mother on that side of the bed. From my shoulders down to my waist, I felt something being pushed in and out at the same time. The feeling was inexplicable and made me feel really uneasy. I just wanted to move out. Mom was beside me, and we sat out for a long time and chanted *Hanuman Chalisa*—all the *shlokas* in the world that I knew of. Call me old-fashioned, but it really gives me strength. The fear of the unknown is the worst. I continued chanting while I prayed for relief, all the while wondering why my grandmother's soul would make me go through this. My mom made green tea in the kitchen while she handed me an iron tool, believing it would keep any negative energy away. But the feeling kept coming and going, and I breathed hard and exhaled with my mouth, which seemed to be the only thing distracting me from the alien feelings inside me.

I was growing tired of it and desperately praying for relief. This went on for another three hours until it was 6:00 a.m. in the morning and some natural light seeped into the house along with other members of the household waking up. I felt relieved, and the alien feeling disappeared as soon as I was surrounded by them, and the tired me let out five to six yawns. But I felt exhausted from the inside out and sleep-deprived too.

While everyone was going through their morning routine, I sat there, a little shaken, seeking my mom and asking her to be near, as being alone spooked me. The fear just wrapped me completely, as there was no logical explanation for this, and the illogical one was scary. Was it her spirit? Just like in movies, it got active after 3:00 a.m. Every horror story revolved in my head, and I could find similarities that scared me even more.

Somehow my mom built up the courage to tell the other members of the family, and I joined in and narrated the events of the last night. One or two had noticed us when they woke up to go to the washroom. After hearing this, they seemed concerned for my well-being and informed me that this was why no one was sleeping there. How was I to explain to them that, physically, I was absolutely fine but, mentally, I was terrified? As each of them found out my truth, they took a few steps to make things better by lighting *agarbattis* in that room. They were all worried about what happened and its impact on me. I could see their puzzled faces and couldn't help but wonder how clueless we are about anything that is beyond us—the limitations of the human mind!

This whole experience left me with so many questions that still remain unanswered. But again, when I told my sister about it, she told me that my mind was playing games with me. Somehow that one line stuck with me, and I mentally retraced every moment of that night to understand the hows and whys. Before I slept there, an elderly relative had warned me about sleeping there. So subconsciously, it could have registered in my mind. And when I woke up at 3:00 a.m. feeling cold, I was actually cold, but the timing just psyched my mind, and my body started getting weird sensations. And the fear did not leave me for hours, as it was dark at night, and everyone was asleep.

Somehow, the assumption that my mind was playing games helped me explain the puzzling night. And as soon as I had a logical explanation for it, my fear began to fade day by day. I wish I had met my sister a few days earlier and heard this. I could have saved myself from all those sleepless nights that I stayed awake, fearing that if I slept, I might experience the same thing after 3:00 a.m. And look at how evil the mind can be. Even if I managed to fall asleep early, every night I woke up around 3:00 a.m., and then I had to wake my husband up and hold him close, watch some series on my phone to distract myself, and then sleep until the next morning. But once I realized the games of my mind, I was at ease, and things only got better from there.

Today, I have conquered that fear. Every day, I retrained my mind to believe it was all a game and had nothing to do with my grandmother's spirit. I want to convey this to everyone: 'Respect nature, its forces, its positives and negatives, and the experience of your ancestors.' Sometimes you can step back so that you don't need to go through these difficult times to understand it all.

I had to break the stereotype of my mind that got me to believe in superstitions and channel my thoughts into believing the logical explanation. It was a struggle and many nights of hard work, but I did it. I realized through this that it's easier to fight the stereotypes that exist in our society than to fight the stereotypes that develop in our minds from what we hear or see in movies. All these things have a profound impact on us, and training our minds to go against them is the toughest battle.

Even today, my heart sometimes tells me it was my grandmother hugging and bidding goodbye to me one last time, a sweet thought that I don't let my mind believe. I can't let that fear come back into my life—the fear of the unknown—that made me so weak. Fear handicaps your mind, and no matter what the truth of that night is, I want to believe the theory that makes me strong and positive.

*****

Author's Message

I believe we need to fight our inner battles if we want to eradicate any superstitions from a society that cripples our minds and stops us from living life fully.

35

ENGLISH: IS IT A NECESSARY EVIL?

Swati Verma

Children are pure souls. They are born into a world where they see adults judge and stereotype other people. They follow in their footsteps to eventually become the same people. As they grow up and step out into their second home, which is school, they start absorbing everything around them. Their knowledge and beliefs are influenced by their surroundings, friends, teachers, and books. The company they keep teaches them more and helps them form their perceptions about the world and the people they meet. One such perception is the superiority of English speakers over Hindi speakers. And this difference can be felt most when you transfer from a Hindi-medium school to an English-medium school. Though I was already exposed to regionalism as a north Indian growing up in the southern state of Kerala, its impact was less than what I faced when I joined a convent with a below-average command over the English language.

India does have a national language, Hindi, but knowing it alone is never enough to stay ahead in any competition. One has to be affluent in English too; one might as well say that one can afford to not know Hindi, but knowing English is a must if one wants to be counted among the rich and successful. Lord Macaulay's reformed education system has given rise to a whole new generation of Macaulay's children who worship Western culture and respect the English language more than their own mother tongue. People feel shame for not knowing English and are often ridiculed for it. Although fluent English speakers account for only 10.62%[1] of the total Indian population, the number of coaching centres and online courses teaching fluent English is increasing year after year. This demonstrates the growing need for people in this country to learn this language in order to survive in the highly competitive world we live in. Speaking English has become a symbol of status and, unfortunately, a benchmark for the literate. This stereotype of the supremacy of English-speaking people has seeped so deeply into the minds of our people that even children have become slaves to these thoughts, which reflect in their actions. Hailing from a Hindi-medium government school, my admission into an English convent made me a victim of this type of stereotype.

In the convent, it was compulsory to talk in English. As if that wasn't enough for a newcomer like me, I became a soft target for bullies in my class. I remember some of my classmates using heavy words in their sentences, and they would turn to me and ask for their meanings. They found it amusing to observe my confusion. Struggling to fit in as an outsider among them was already a very big challenge, as neither the language nor the culture or family or lifestyle shared any similarities, and hence that left me with only topics pertaining to our subjects and exams. But even that was discussed in fluent English, whereas I had learned all this with Hindi terminologies and broken English.

And this was just the beginning of a few months of restlessness and failure. The lectures by teachers were also purely in English, and the subjects that I learned with Hindi terminologies were now all spoken and written in English. Fortunately, my mother had studied in a convent, and she could translate it all for me. It took me some time to catch up, but like a tortoise in a race against a rabbit, I kept crawling

---

[1] Wikipedia contributors. (2023, February 24). List of countries by English-speaking population. Wikipedia.

my way ahead. But the race was long and hard. Even when I could understand the lectures of my teachers and grasp everything they taught, I could never communicate with them effectively or answer my question papers well if I did not learn how to speak and write English. And here, I got help from a grammar book that was just part of the syllabi for everyone else, but for me, it was a lifesaver in the form of "Wren and Martin". This book laid the foundation of the English language in my mind. I lived with this book for one whole year, read it all the time, and practised it more than any other subject. I even read a few English mystery novels from my school library like Nancy Drew and The Hardy Boys to learn how to speak this language, which had become a necessary evil for me.

I was used to being among the best in my class, but now I was being counted among the last, and I really wanted to change that. Every insult thrown at me I brushed aside because I could not retaliate in the same way. With each failure, I focused on improving where I was lacking with each obstacle. It was easier to focus on me than on everything around me. This tortoise, too, had to keep moving slowly and steadily towards her goal. I would try to talk in English often, like my peers and like my teachers. I would fumble, pronounce a word wrongly, or make mistakes often, but in the form of ridicule by peers or sometimes through my teachers; I would learn where I went wrong and correct it immediately. This went on for months, and finally, the day came when I reached the finish line. A girl who, a year ago, could not even frame a full sentence in English was today the top student in English. She could speak fluently, even better than many in her class. My classmates could not believe their eyes, and they took turns checking my paper to verify if there was some mistake in the evaluation. But I'd had enough of failing. And my victories were not confined to just my academics.

Creativity had always been a very important aspect of my schooling. My mother always encouraged me to participate in extracurricular activities at school, and I would win prizes and accolades every year. But until that year, it was only in my mother tongue, Hindi. That changed when I beat my classmates even in English recitation, elocution, and essay-writing competitions. This was the first time I was victorious in each of these categories, both in Hindi and English. My command of the language had greatly improved over the course of the year. Hard work really paid off, and I was successful in becoming the best again. I surpassed even the ones who flaunted their diction and vocabulary in the class. This was a solid response to every mockery and failure of the previous year. I'd evolved into this new, confident person who believes she can accomplish anything if she puts her mind to it. And now everyone wanted to be my friend. They looked up at me. I had regained my position as one of the best in my class. My grades got so much better, and my confidence level heightened.

Though it was the toughest year of my life, I can never forget the transition and the fight in me to excel in any environment. And it's only gotten better from there. And now, when I look back, I realize how things worked out for the best. My earlier years in a Hindi-medium school gave me a good base in my mother tongue, such a strong foundation that I can write Hindi in its own script and not just in English, or as we commonly say, "Hinglish". In Macaulay's world of education, not many can write Hindi like Hindi, and people seem impressed when I do that with ease.

So, to anyone who feels inferior because they attend Hindi-medium or government schools, I would say: 'It's up to you how you project yourself.' English has definitely become a language of status in society, but you learn it for your own growth, not to meet the standards of society or show your superiority. I have nothing against the language. English has brought the whole world closer by opening the door to communication among nations. It's a convenient and friendly language. But it becomes a necessary evil for those who don't know this language. Even today, many places don't have a formal education in this language, which limits the scope of the people living there. And through no fault of their own, these people are looked down upon or ridiculed for not knowing the language. And the worst part is when their talent or intelligence is overlooked if they cannot speak English properly. And average intelligence is put on a high pedestal if expressed with fancy words and scientific terminologies in English. The status symbol that English brings has created a scenario where ideas or thoughts are realized and accepted more if expressed in English. This has made this language a necessary evil for many, as it was for me for that whole year in school.

But all I can say is that it humbled me to experience this, and I empathize with people who are struggling with this language. So, through this article, I'd like to encourage them to never let anyone tell them they're less than others. And it's good to learn this language, but only for your own self-development. Let's not learn it to establish any supremacy over others or to meet the social standards of the smart or the intelligent. Don't look down upon others, and don't take it from anyone. This was my small attempt to fight against a stereotype that people have, and I believe that one should always strive to break such stereotypes and shatter these boxes in order to live in a more equal society.

*****

Author's Message

Every time someone tries to make you feel less, just remind yourself that the tortoise wins the race in the end.

MEET THE AUTHORS

Akhila Mohan CG

Akhila Mohan CG is an award-winning poet and writer, and researcher, currently based in Bengaluru, India. More than fifty of her creative write-ups have been published in national and international literary journals, anthologies, and platforms, including Unstamatic, TMYS Review, Scarlet Dragonfly, Whiptail Journal, Failed Haiku, Juggernaut, Readomania, and others. Tamarind: Sweet and Sour Poems about Love, Loss, Longing, and Life, published by Kitaab, is her debut poetry collection. She is the recipient of the P.B. Shelley: Youth's Unextinguished Fire International Poetry Award (2021). She is the co-founder of a creative firm, ArtLit: An Art and Literary Community.

Anuradha Gupta

Anuradha Gupta is an educator from Gurgaon who currently manages quality assurance for a coding education firm. Though she began her career with risk consulting, she later forayed into "training and education" after a six-year corporate stint. Today, she is not only committed to learning and writing more but also

nurtures the lives of school students by sharing her knowledge of creative writing with them. During her leisure time, she loves to sing, listen to music, watch movies, and read books. If you'd like to get in touch with Anuradha, you can reach out to her through her Instagram handle @anuradha_gupta2706.

Awantika Gupta

Creation and fiction are two words Awantika holds very dear and close to her. She has created several fictional characters who play the roles of villains, heroes, and heroines and portray the emotions of friendship, love, trust, hope, achievement, and loss, to name a few. With her sheer imagination for background, locations, houses, and key moments in her stories and screenplays, she tries to embed these characters' real-life psyches into their fictional ones. Awantika Gupta is also a journalism student with six years of professional experience. She loves visualization and wants others to see it through her novel in the future.

Author Neelima

Author Neelima hails from a small town in India. She has garnered much of her acclaim for her initial work, "A Beauty by Its Blue Reflection", published in 2021. When she is not writing on her favourite couch, she is a proud NITian and a working engineer at one of the biggest MNCs in India. As framed by an engineer,  Neelima's life is a little logical and more magical. Neelima spends much of her time traveling, meditating, visiting the local monuments, and catching up with her favourite rom-coms, thrillers, sci-fi movies, and music. As an admitted movie fanatic, she feeds her addiction by catching up with new Bollywood soaps, science documentaries, and autobiographies every weekend. Altogether, she is an explorer who loves to enjoy new things in her own world full of gadgets. She also believes in karma and the path to Nirvana.

Aruna Parandhama

Aruna Parandhama is a passionate educator from Bangalore. She found her calling in teaching and writing after working for an imminent corporate company. She is the published author of a short story and several poems. She moonlights as a freelance content writer and a voice-over artist. She is an avid reader and enjoys debating, mentoring, and training adolescent students.

Bhumika Kukreja

Bhumika is an MBA and is currently working towards her CFA charter. She has been working in the corporate sector for four years and has a passion for writing too. She also holds a diploma in creative writing from IGNOU. Bhumika was born and brought up in Delhi, and she believes in women's potential. She is a self-motivated individual who is into writing articles, stories, and poetry.

Charvi Jain

Charvi is an avid reader who adores thrilling horror stories but also cherishes a good rom-com. Based in Bangalore, she's paving her way to become a psychologist. Her hobbies range from learning new languages to sketching her feelings away. She's got a dramatic flair when expressing herself but prefers to make lemonade out of the lemons thrown her way.

Crrystal Agravat

Crrystal Agravat is a twenty-five-year-old writer who found her way through the complicated field of psychology. Her fairy-tale-inspired childhood gave her a chance to construct little artworks. Her creative imagination provided her the platform to express her thoughts in the most beguiling way possible. Inspired by Emily  Dickinson, Maya Angelou, and Rupi Kaur, her world revolves around poetry. Her undying love for writing and expressing thoughts on paper led her to make her debut in the world of poets. Her poems mainly focus on sadness, love, betrayal, and hope. To her, writing is like the freedom a slave experiences after its banishment. In simpler terms, writing is a part of her essential existence.

Darshana Sontakke

 Darshana Sontakke is a young, self-driven storyteller and creative content writer hailing from the holy city of Ujjain. She addresses herself as a light worker, and her broomstick is her pen. Writing is her calling, which began in 2018 when she wrote and published extraordinary real-life inspirational stories. She was featured in the local newspapers and on websites for this initiative. She has also worked as a freelance content writer for media companies and events featuring Bollywood celebrities. Further, she believes that at the end of the day, we are all stories—why not be an exceptional one? You can connect with her on Instagram @idarshanasontakke.

Dr Janki Mistry

Dr Janki Mistry is an Associate Professor of Finance at the Department of Business, Industrial, and Management, Veer Narmad South Gujarat University, Surat. She has an MBA degree in finance from Veer Narmad University in South Gujarat and a doctorate in management. She has published around thirty-five papers in national and international journals and has authored three books. She has also translated a novel from Gujarati to English. She also serves on the board of Infina Finance Private Limited as an independent director.

Juhi Arya

Juhi Arya has specialized in social work since earning her M.A degree in public policy and governance from the Tata Institute of Social Sciences. Juhi has spent her career working with communities and has multi-stakeholder engagement with more than three years of work experience in the field of corporate social responsibility. Under CSR, she has been working on promoting preventive health care, sanitation, and making available safe drinking water; promoting education, the environment, and sustainability; protecting animal welfare and cultural heritage; and involving herself in extensive field work and day-to-day community consultation. In addition, Juhi has a keen interest in reading, visiting historical monuments, keeping a diary, and playing sports.

Irene Munyiri

Irene Munyiri is a law student in Nairobi, Kenya. She is a writer, and her number one slogan is that life is too short to read boring books. She loves to keep her writers entertained with her sense of humour. When not writing, she loves to spend her time with family and travel. She is always cheerful and optimistic about life. She is  very enthusiastic about everything but a terrible dancer! She loves to be creative and make the most of her life.

Karen

The author has done her BMM (advertising) and is an advanced graphic designer. She has struggled with a learning disability. In spite of various setbacks in life, she has overcome all obstacles with a positive attitude of never giving up!

Kirti S. Wadhwa

Kirti S. Wadhwa is a researcher, nutritionist, and writer. She has been creating awareness about health among her readers through her articles for two years. Then she decided to move on to other uncomfortable issues that society grapples with but shies away from exploring. Kirti has a uniquely wry voice  that shines through her work. The rawness in her writing evokes a spectrum of emotions that readers can feel and relate to. She lives in New Delhi with her mother and two younger brothers. She can be reached at wadhwakirti915@gmail.com.

Limakshi Devi

Limakshi Devi is a thinker (over-thinker at times), writer, avid reader, loving daughter, caring sister, understanding partner, and passionate human. She is a wordsmith by passion and profession. Working in a corporate environment as a content and copywriter during the weekdays and finding herself lost in her garden amidst the magic of nature during the weekends, she tries to maintain the balance between life and living.

Niyati Singh

Niyati is a first-year student pursuing her graduation. But that is not the only thing that defines her. She is a writer who seeks stories and is often found unwinding at Irani Café. At this place, she musters the courage to seek out the story of the cafe's owner. But she is not there only for stories but also for the delicious chicken keema.

Niyati is a soul who is up for conversations until it's not small talk. She is often found walking alone and exploring the world on her feet in collaboration with Google Maps.

Pernel

The author is an academic coordinator, a high school teacher teaching English (literature) and social sciences, and a career counsellor. She has been an avid reader right from childhood and has a positive attitude towards life. She is a torchbearer of feminism. Her hobbies are reading, cooking, travelling, adventure, and sports.

Ridima Vaidya

Ridima, an artist at heart, is based in Canada. Stories, poems, ginger tea, theatre, dance, movies, chats, friends, and family sum her up. A simple girl who lives her ordinary life quite extraordinarily.

Swati Verma

Writer at heart, creative by experience, and engineer by education—a perfect mix! This is Swati Verma, and her journey is described in one sentence. The variety of roles she has lived through play a pivotal role in shaping the person she is today, which perfectly seeps into her writing too. Though she hails from the beautiful hills of Kerala, higher education and work made her move away from this heavenly abode. Having moved across the country, she found her second home in the city of dreams, Mumbai, where she found the wings to express her thoughts and discovered her passion for writing.

Tulsi Nambiar

Tulsi is a high school student who has published multiple stories in different anthologies. She took up her passion for writing during the COVID-19 period. She is keen to develop her own style of writing and is in the process of doing so.

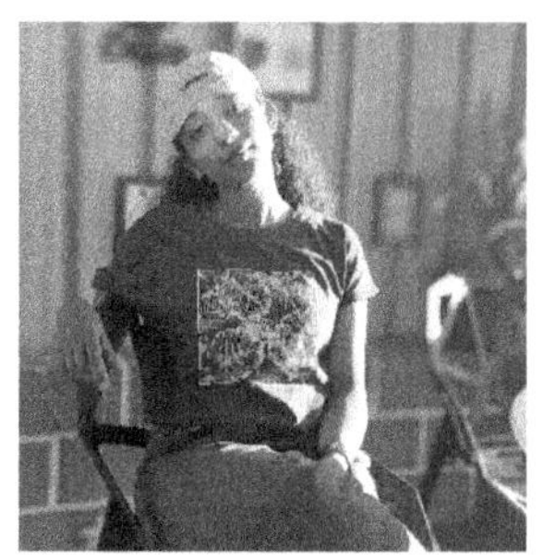

Uma Iyer

Uma Iyer is a blogger and a writer from Pune, India. She is one of the best-known short story writers on the blogging portal Momspresso. She has been featured in many live sessions as a winner of their famous hundred-word short story contests. Uma is also a story, screenplay, and dialogue writer for short films, feature films, and web series. Her first short film, titled "The Third Eye", won several nominations and recognitions at various international film festivals across the world.

V. Rashmi Rao

V. Rashmi Rao is a creative content writer and digital marketing expert who excels at creating exceptional content across various platforms, both print and digital. Having spent more than twelve years in the industry, she has gained immense knowledge about the market and the audience. She has written several articles,

stories, poems, and technical or web content for clients globally. With an MBA in HR & Operations, Rashmi also holds several certifications in the fields of content writing and digital marketing. She believes the right content can influence people in the right way. When Rashmi isn't writing, you may find her painting, dancing, or admiring art.

Vaishnavi. S

Vaishnavi is a social worker specializing in mental health. She is committed to supporting individuals and communities in achieving holistic wellness. A dedicated queer ally and advocate for LGBTQIA+ rights, she is passionate about fostering social justice, equity, and inclusion.

Vinay Damodar

Vinay Damodar is a senior Ph.D. scholar at the Tata Institute of Social Sciences, Mumbai. He has a B.A. in Social Sciences and an M.A. in Social Work with a specialization in Community Organization and Development Practice. He also has an M.Phil. in Inclusive Development and Social Justice. He has

worked with Nikhil Dey and Aruna Roy at Majdoor Kisan Shakti Sanghatan (MKSS). He has written extensive scholarly articles in English and Marathi in Round Table India, Youth ki Aawaz, The Print, Prabuddha Bharat Newsletter, and Shikshan Sanshodhan Journal of Arts, Humanities, and Social Sciences, etc.

We love creating beautiful books for you!

Come be a part of our ever-growing community of authors.
Grow, write, and publish with us!

Scan here to explore
books, authors and more

Connect with us on socials. We'd love to hear from you!

    Inkfeathers Publishing

www.ingramcontent.com/pod-product-compliance
Lightning Source LLC
Chambersburg PA
CBHW071736150726
47998CB00005B/1667